HISTORICAL CATASTROPHES: FLOODS

⋏ Addison-Wesley

AN ADDISONIAN PRESS BOOK

by Walter R. Brown and Billye W. Cutchen

HISTORICAL CATASTROPHES:
FLOODS

Titles in the Historical Catastrophe Series

Wood engraving on preceding two pages:
Flood of the Arno River at Florence.

Text Copyright © 1975 by Walter R. Brown and Billye W. Cutchen
Illustrations Copyright © 1975 by Addison-Wesley Publishing Co., Inc.
All Rights Reserved
Addison-Wesley Publishing Company, Inc.
Reading, Massachusetts 01867
Printed in the United States of America

CDEFGHIJK-WZ-7987

Library of Congress Cataloging in Publication Data
Brown, Walter R   1929–
    Historical catastrophes, flood.
    "An Addisonian Press book."
    Includes index.
    SUMMARY: Describes the famous floods of Johnstown,
Florence, Venice, and other areas caused by such conditions as tidal waves, breaking dams, rising rivers, and
hurricanes.
        1. Floods—Juvenile literature. [1. Floods]
    I. Cutchen, Billye W., 1930–   joint author
    II. Title.
    GB1205.B76   904'.5   74-23684
    ISBN 0-201-00762-2

CONTENTS

CENTRAL ARKANSAS LIBRARY SYSTEM
LITTLE ROCK PUBLIC LIBRARY
700 LOUISIANA STREET
LITTLE ROCK, ARKANSAS 72201

CHAPTER ONE

WATER AND MAN

WATER PLAYS MANY ROLES in our lives. We swim in it, go boating, wash with it. It is necessary to all life processes we know about, both plant and animal. In fact, next to oxygen man needs it more than any other substance just to stay alive.

Man has always had to consider whether or not water was available before he could settle in any new place. He and his animals needed it to drink. It was necessary for his crops to grow. Water power can run machinery and even produce electricity. It has often provided a mode of transportation for man. That is why it is not uncommon to see cities located along rivers and lakeshores and around sea-ports.

Because man needs water, he often lives in places that are not safe. For water is not always kind to man. Sometimes there is more water than man needs—so much that it destroys man's crops and homes and even man himself.

If we look at the earliest writings of man and study his myths, we find that he has always been concerned about floods. Almost every group of early people had a story of an ancient flood in which only one person or one family was saved from drowning.

The early Greeks had a myth about Phaeton, who drove the chariot of his father, the sun, too close to the earth. The earth caught fire and Zeus decided he would flood the earth to put out the fire. He advised Deucalion to build a chest for himself and his wife, Pyrrha, to float in until the flood waters subsided.

After the rains had stopped, they floated around for nine days, and finally Deucalion and Pyrrha landed on top of Mt. Parnassus. They were so grateful to be alive that they found a temple and offered up prayers. But they were sad that there were no other people alive. A voice told them to cast behind them the bones of their mother. This shocked them until they interpreted the meaning of "mother" to be the earth. When they tossed rocks (the bones of the earth) over their shoulders, people took form where each of the rocks hit the ground.

One artist's idea of what Noah's Ark looked like (1494).

Other stories of worldwide floods are in the legends of the Egyptians, the Persians, the Hindus, the Indians of the Western Hemisphere, and many others. The Araucanians of South America tell of a great deluge in which they were saved by the tip of a very tall hill. The North American Creek Indians tell a story of a dog who warned his master to make a raft because everything was to be covered by flooding water. The man and his dog were the only beings saved.

Of course, we know the Biblical story of Noah and the Ark. Noah, his family, and two of every kind of animal lived on the Ark for one year and 11 days while the earth was flooded. You can read the details of this event in the book of Genesis.

Today, man is still concerned about floods. But instead of believing they are caused by wrathful gods, we study the weather conditions that cause the various kinds of floods. We try to see what can be done to prevent deaths and protect our property.

We see regular river flooding, such as happens almost yearly on our mighty Mississippi and less often on the Arno River in Italy. We read about catastrophic sea floods, such as the one that hit the coast of Holland during the winter of 1953. This flood was caused by a gale-force wind that was blowing inland at high tide, causing the dikes to break. Two thousand people were drowned and 600 square miles of farmlands were flooded with salt water. Another kind of sea flood is caused by tidal waves, or Tsunamis.

In this book we shall retell some modern-day stories of floods. You will read of the terror people feel when they find their belongings and even their lives in danger. In these stories, water is a destroyer. Its force can be so vast that man has trouble just imagining it, much less coping with it. But you will also be reminded of the fact that water is one of our most valuable resources and becomes a destroyer only when man's greed or stupidity leads him to misuse it.

You will also read of man's willingness to help his neighbor when there is trouble. People who have never met the victims of floods lend a helping hand. Usually, there are even people from other communities who come to their aid. And as men who were strangers work side by side to repair and rebuild communities, they become aware of their need for each other.

CHAPTER TWO

THE JOHNSTOWN FLOOD 1889

CAN YOU IMAGINE a wall of water nearly as high as a four-story building rushing down a narrow valley toward your home? This is what the people who lived in Johnstown, Pennsylvania, saw on May 31, 1889. That terrible rush of water killed more than 2,000 people in less than an hour.

This disaster was caused by the breaking of a dam that stood about 14 miles up the valley from Johnstown. It was a huge dam—the largest one in the world that was made mostly of dirt. And it held back twenty-five million tons of water. As usually happens, this flood began with a heavy rain. Water poured into the lake from the steep-sided mountains, causing the amount of water behind the dam to grow until the pressure became too great for the dam to hold. The center of the dam washed away and within an hour twenty-five million tons of water smashed down the valley, sweeping almost everything in its path away and killing approximately one person out of every ten who lived there.

The story of the Johnstown flood began long before the rains did. Part of the story began millions of years ago, with the creation of the Allegheny Mountains. Although rugged and deeply cut by swiftly flowing streams, these mountains are not very high. The top of Mt. Davis is only 3,213 feet above sea level, and it is the highest point in Pennsylvania.

Traveling through these rough mountains during the early days of this country's history was a difficult job. The jolting stagecoach ride between Philadelphia and Pittsburgh took several uncomfortable days to complete. So the second beginning of the Johnstown flood story was in 1824 when the State of Pennsylvania began to build a series of canals and railways between the two cities. In the mid-1800's, the trip from Philadelphia to Pittsburgh was a long one. Travelers went westward from Philadelphia in a railway car pulled by horses until they reached the Susquehanna River. They then boarded a boat and traveled to Hollidaysburg on the Susquehanna and Juniata Rivers. Another short stretch of horse-drawn railway carried them to Johnstown.

The last hundred miles between Johnstown and Pittsburgh proved to be a problem. A canal had to be dug between the two cities and a steady supply of water had to be provided to be certain that the barges could move at any time of the year. And so it was for this reason that the dam that was to later destroy Johnstown was built.

The engineers in charge of the project chose a narrow part of the deep valley that had been cut by the South Fork Creek. This was a short distance above where the creek flowed into the Little Conemaugh River and only 14 miles upstream from the canal that began at Johnstown. After twelve years of work the job was finished, and the men who had built the dam were proud of the job they had done. The dam was made of stone with dirt piled on top. Over this was a thick layer of loose rock. It stood more than 100 feet above the old creek bed and was 272 feet thick at its base. The top of the dam was more than 900 feet long. The flow of water from the huge lake that lay behind the dam was controlled by valves that could be opened to let water flow through five outlet pipes. To protect the dam from too much water in the lake, a spillway ten feet deep and 70 feet wide was cut into the solid rock around the eastern end of the dam.

Finally the last link in the canal-railway system between the two great cities was complete. Passengers and freight arrived almost daily at the terminal in Johnstown, and the lake behind the dam on South Fork Creek supplied the canal with a steady supply of water.

There was another event—one that took place even before the dam was started—that set the stage for the terrible flood at Johnstown. It was the invention of the steam locomotive.

In 1814, an Englishman built a steam engine that pulled a train of eight cars at a speed of four miles an hour. Sixteen years later the South Carolina Railroad began its first regularly scheduled run. By 1850, two years before the Johnstown canal dam was completed, the State of Pennsylvania began replacing horse-drawn railways with steam-driven trains. And, in 1854, tracks were laid across the mountains between Johnstown and Pittsburgh, and the canal was abandoned. No longer needed, the huge dam on the South Fork Creek was almost forgotten. Heavy rains and high water ate into the protecting rocks and through the dirt fill. The dam became weaker and weaker.

In 1889, Memorial Day was celebrated on May 30. It was a day on which the people of Johnstown remembered those men who had died during the Civil War. The town was decorated with flowers and flags and, with all of the businesses closed, the streets were lined with people. A parade of bands and veterans marched through the streets and then to the cemetery by the river. The rain did not begin that day until nearly three in the afternoon, when most of the ceremonies had been finished. For most of the citizens of Johnstown it had been a relaxed and happy holiday.

It was a good time to live and work in Johnstown. The building of the canal nearly 40 years before had started the sleepy little town on its way to becoming a big city. Its first steel mill was built in 1850 and the need for steel during the Civil War and afterward as the West began to open up turned the little canal terminal into an industrial city.

It was not a pretty place in 1889, however. Johnstown itself lay in the flat land where the Little Conemaugh River and Stony Creek came together to form the Conemaugh River. Steel mills lined the rivers in all directions from the town and clouds of yellowish-smoke usually filled the air of the narrow valleys. But the surrounding mountains were still covered with heavy forests where bear, wildcats, pheasants, grouse, and turkeys could be hunted.

It was the rugged beauty of the mountains around Johnstown that caused a group of wealthy men from Pittsburgh to buy the lake on South Fork Creek in 1879. For the next ten years these men were busy building cabins and boat docks along the shores of the lake, which they now called Lake Conemaugh. For two weeks or so every summer, they came with their families to escape from the heat and smoke of Pittsburgh to walk, hunt, and fish in the beautiful Allegheny Mountains.

The new owners of Lake Conemaugh found that the dam that held back the waters of their lake was in poor condition. Very few repairs had been done during the 25 years since the canal had been abandoned. Many people who lived in the valleys below the dam hoped that the members of the new "South Fork Fishing and Hunting Club" would rebuild the dam. Among these worried citizens of

Johnstown were the owners of the Cambria Iron Works. The company had invested about fifty million dollars in the steel mills, and the owners knew that if the dam broke the company might be ruined. So the president of the company sent one of his engineers to look at the dam.

The report of the condition of the dam was not a good one. The engineer reported that a small break in the dam, caused by a storm in 1862, had been repaired by filling the hole with tree stumps, branches, and sand. The engineer felt that if the lake were to ever fill completely, this weak place might give way again. He also discovered that the valves that operated the discharge pipes had rusted shut and that there was no way to lower the level of the water behind the dam.

This report was sent to the new owners of the lake in November of 1880. But the report was ignored. Instead of trying to repair the dam, the Club spent its money on stocking the lake with fish. Then they partly blocked the overflow channel around the end of the dam with nets that would keep their fish from escaping into the river below. To make the situation even worse, they lowered the height of the dam several feet to make it wide enough for a road to be built across its top. To do this, they had to put huge poles into the overflow channel for support for a bridge. As a result, the channel that was meant to allow extra water to escape from the lake if it got too high was partly blocked.

But on Memorial Day, 1889, the dam was still standing and most of the people of Johnstown had forgotten the warnings of the steel company's engineer. The dam had held this long, they figured, so perhaps the men who owned the Fishing and Hunting Club had been right after all. So when the rain began that afternoon, few people in the valley were concerned about the dam breaking.

They were concerned about the rain, however. It fell in solid sheets of cold water all night. Eleven inches of rain had fallen in May, on soil that was already soaked by the sudden melting of 14 inches of snow the month before. The rivers were bank-full, and the lake above the town had filled to the point where tons of water were rushing through the partly blocked overflow channel.

The next day was a Friday, and the men reported for work at the steel mills and railroad yards as usual. A heavy mist hung over the city and the sky was dark with clouds at dawn. Buckets that had been left out overnight were found to hold eight inches of rainwater. Water from the rivers began creeping slowly up the streets and into the buildings.

Spring floods were nothing new to Johnstown, but everyone seemed to know that this was going to be a bad one. The Cambria Mill sent its men home to take care of their families. By mid-morning the other businesses began to close. Main Street and the floors of the steel mills were covered by swirling, muddy water. One man had already drowned when he accidentally drove his wagon into a water-filled ditch.

By noon the Little Conemaugh River and Stony Creek were rising rapidly. Rowboats made their way up and down the flooded streets, taking stranded families to higher ground. Two bridges had collapsed and washed away. Many people decided to give up fighting the water that was rising at nearly a foot an hour and moved to the hills around the town. But most of the citizens of the valleys stayed with their property, moving furniture and other valuables to the upper floors of their homes. The daily passenger train, on its way from Pittsburgh to Philadelphia with 50 passengers aboard, passed through Johnstown only to be stopped three miles up the valley by a landslide that had blocked the tracks.

At the dam men were working frantically. Water was rushing through the overflow spillway more than seven feet deep, and the men knew that they had to remove the iron nets that partly blocked the water. But the nets were solidly set and now were clogged with debris. Slowly the water rose toward the top of the dam. Huge spurts of water came from leaks along the face of the dirt wall. A telegraph message was sent down the valley warning that the dam might not hold.

Shortly before noon, the lake began to pour over the top of the dam in a huge sheet of water. At a little after three o'clock, the dam gave way with a terrible roar. A young boy who was watching from a nearby hillside later recalled that the dam,

". . . seemed to push out all at once. Not a break. Just one big push."

Twenty-five million tons of water poured out and within less than an hour the lake was empty. A wall of water, sometimes 30 to 40 feet high, rushed down the narrow valley. Trees were uprooted and swept along. Huge rocks were torn from the ground. A farm was washed away, and the splinters of its buildings added to the mass of debris carried by the flood.

The village of South Fork was the first of several towns that stood in the path of the flood. This little cluster of houses lay in the flat land where the Little Conemaugh River blended with the South Fork Creek. Fortunately, most of its houses were either on high ground or were up the Little Conemaugh valley far enough to escape. Only two people drowned and about two-dozen houses were carried away.

A few miles farther downstream stood a stone bridge over which ran the tracks of the Pennsylvania Railroad. The debris being carried by the flood waters jammed in the narrow passage under the bridge and, for a few moments, the water was blocked. Then the stone of the bridge suddenly gave way, and the wall of water continued down the valley, now even higher than before.

Below the bridge was a telegraph tower. By now, its lines were dead and the operator had little warning of the disaster that was rushing down toward him. He heard the thundering of the water and, from his perch high above the ground, he saw the crest of the flood. Below him an engine waited with full steam up. The operator shouted a warning to the engineer, John Hess.

"The dam's broken!" he screamed. "Clear out, or you will be washed off the tracks!"

Quickly, Hess backed his engine down the tracks toward the town of East Conemaugh, where his family was. Hoping to warn as many people as possible, he tied down the whistle of his engine.

The shrieking engine passed Mineral Point, a tiny village that stood on the north bank of the river. But the flood waters were too close for the warning to do much good. All 32 of the houses in the village and 16 of its inhabitants were swept away within seconds after he passed.

But the sound of the engine's whistle reached the people of East Conemaugh, six miles downstream from Mineral Point, before the water did. Hess and the engine he was driving won the race with the wall of water with enough time to spare for the engineer to jump from the engine's cab, run to his home, gather up his family, and lead them to safety.

One of the people who heard the steady whistle of Hess' engine was the conductor of the express passenger train that had been stopped shortly after noon by blocked tracks. For the past three hours, he had watched anxiously as the river nearby slowly left its banks and crept closer to the tracks. He felt responsible for the comfort and safety of the 50 passengers on the train. When a small bridge across the river washed away, the conductor had walked through the train, trying to reassure the frightened people. He did not tell them that the yardmaster had told him of the telegraphed warning that the dam above the town was leaking badly. After all, there was little that could be done. Landslides and high water now blocked the tracks in both directions. The train and its passengers were trapped in the yards at East Conemaugh.

When he heard the whistle of the engine echoing down the valley, he realized immediately what it meant. Quickly he called the porters and brakemen together and told them to get the passengers off the train and up into the hills.

One of the passengers was Reverend T. H. Robinson. He, too, heard the shrill whistle, but did not know what it meant. He looked out of the window and saw what looked at first like a huge pile of rubbish—trees, brush, and rocks—moving slowly down the valley. Then he realized that what he was seeing was a 40-foot-high bank of muddy water. The front edge of the flood was still several hundred yards away and moving fairly slowly.

Reverend Robinson shouted a warning to the other passengers at about the same time as did the conductor, who was running along outside the train.

"Get to the hills! Get to the hills!" The shouted warning traveled through the train quickly. "Run for your lives!"

For a moment everyone sat quietly, frozen with fear. Then all of the passengers in the car jumped to their feet and rushed for the doors.

A 40-foot high wall of water crushed the houses of Johnstown like they were paper. Many people died in the fire in the debris that had washed against the railroad bridge.

The train had been split into two sections and parked side-by-side on the tracks. The car in which Reverend Robinson was a passenger was in the section farther away from the town and the hills beyond. When they climbed from the car, they found their path to safety blocked by the second section of the train. Only three choices seemed open to them. They could climb between the cars of the other train, crawl under, or run around the back of the last car. Bewildered by the confusion, their minds numbed by fear, several people went back into the railroad car that they had just left.

Reverend Robinson made his choice quickly. He ran toward the back end of the train as fast as he could. He soon reached the last car, ran behind it, and crossed the tracks. A ditch, full of tumbling water, blocked his path. He looked up the valley at the mass of water and debris that was roaring down toward him and knew that he had only a few seconds to find a way across the ditch. He pulled his eyes away from the approaching flood and studied the ditch in front of him. There, a little distance down the valley, was a small bridge made of a single board laid across from bank to bank. With the muddy water lapping at his feet, Reverend Robinson ran across the board, up the slippery slope, and into the town.

Most of the other passengers of the train were not this lucky. Crawling through or under the second row of railway cars, they found their way blocked by the ditch. Some of the men managed to jump the swirling water, and then turned to help the women who could not jump far enough. Many were pulled to safety, but others were carried away and drowned.

Once across the ditch and over the embankment, they found the streets of the town full of frightened people. Together they ran toward the safety of higher ground. They finally stopped and turned to watch the horrifying sight below.

The wall of water, now perhaps 40 feet high, smashed down onto the tops of the houses that stood closest to the railway yards. They saw houses crushed as if they were made of paper. The two lines of railroad cars tore apart and some of the cars were washed away by the water. Even the heavy engines bobbed around like corks as they were carried down the valley. Of the 50 passengers who had been on the train, fewer than 30 survived. Twenty-eight people from the town were either drowned or crushed by the debris.

After smashing East Conemaugh and its railroad yards, the wave of water moved on down the valley and through the town of Woodvale. Built by the Cambria Iron Company for its employees, it was a pretty little town of clean, white houses, churches, and a few businesses. The 1,000 people who lived there had no warning of the disaster that rushed down on them. One-third of them died when the water struck their homes. After the flood waters went down, only a few houses that had stood along the higher edge of the town were left standing. Two hundred and fifty-five houses had disappeared, along with all of the trees, telegraph poles, and even the railroad tracks.

The advancing water hit the steel mills of the Gautier Wireworks and the boilers burst, sending a towering plume of steam high into the sky. The flood had reached the outskirts of Johnstown. It was now a few minutes after four o'clock, almost an hour since the dam had burst nearly 14 miles away. But few people in the city knew they were in danger.

The water in the rivers that ran through Johnstown seemed to be lowering a little, and many people had started to move their furniture back into the lower floors of their houses. The rain was still falling steadily, but it seemed that the worst of the flood was over. The only warning that they had was a cloud of what looked like dust or smoke moving down the valley toward them. One man later reported that he thought that there had been an explosion of some kind upriver from the town.

The wall of water was now moving so rapidly that its top continuously fell forward, like the crest of a wave on an ocean surf. It carried hundreds of tons of debris that it had gathered from the valley above. The splintered remains of houses and factories, railroad cars and engines, trees and telegraph poles, steel rails and wire, rocks, and the bodies of hundreds of people and animals were carried along, adding to the force of the water. The sound that it made was like the steady roar of thunder. For the next ten minutes the people of Johnstown ran or fought for their lives.

Victor Heiser was 16 years old. He was in the barn that stood behind his home, taking care of the family's horses, when he heard the roar of the coming water. He looked toward the house and saw his father motioning to him from a second-story window. The boy's father had, somehow, figured out the meaning of the strange sounds and cloud that moved down the valley. He was signaling frantically for his son to climb to the top of the stable. Victor did not understand the reason for this strange order, but immediately did what his father told him.

From the top of the barn he watched the water smash through the town. He saw the face of the wall of water curl over and smash down on his home, crushing it like an eggshell, and add its splinters and the bodies of his parents to the mass of debris that it already carried.

The small barn on which he stood was on slightly higher ground than the farmhouse had been and so was missed by the main force of the flood. Instead of being crushed as the house had been, the barn was torn from its foundations and began to roll over and over in the rising water. Desperately, the young man ran and crawled and managed to stay above the water until his raft crashed into a neighbor's house.

Victor then abandoned the barn for the roof of a

still-standing house, and from there managed to leap to the top of a higher, stronger building. But the roof of his new perch was very steep and was made of wooden shingles that were soaked by the long rain. With all of his strength he tried to dig his fingers into the slick wood. He kicked the toes of his shoes into the shingles, trying to dig a toe-hold. But slowly, as he grew more and more tired, he felt himself slipping from the roof. As he slid over the edge of the roof and fell toward the deep water below, he shut his eyes, held his breath, and waited for the cold plunge.

But instead of falling into the swirling water, he landed on something solid. Opening his eyes, he found himself back on the red metal top of his own barn! Now that the most violent part of the flood had passed, the barn floated upright and steady in the rapidly moving water, carrying him swiftly downstream.

Gertrude Quinn's father also guessed the meaning of the distant "thunder" and had shouted to his family to leave the house and run to the hills. Gertrude was only six years old at that time, however, and was taken upstairs by her aunt instead of to the safety of the higher ground. The house was big and made of solid, new brick and, to her aunt, the third floor nursery seemed like the safest place to be in a flood.

But the house collapsed quickly. It gave only one violent shudder and then the brownish water burst through the roof and the floor at the same instant. Gertrude found herself all alone and riding the crest of the flood's wave on top of a mattress that had become jammed into the mass of sodden debris.

The frightened little girl hung onto her raft as it twisted its way down the valley. Other floating debris passed her, some carrying people along. She called for help, but no one answered her. Then the current carried her close to a still-standing building, its roof crowded with people.

One of these was Maxwell McAchren, a worker in the steel mill. Seeing the helpless little girl, he forgot the danger and leaped into the tumbling water. Swimming strongly, he managed to reach the raft and pulled himself up on it. Together they rode alone—the big man comforting the crying, frightened girl.

Below the main part of town, the raft upon which the pair rode suddenly swung toward what was now the shoreline. There they saw a group of men with long poles, trying to reach survivors of the flood as they washed by. One of these was George Skinner, who quickly waded into the water.

"Throw the baby to me!" he called to McAchren. "Throw her here!"

The mill worker did just that. Gertrude was thrown violently across ten feet of the muddy water and into the arms of the waiting Skinner, who carried her to safety. McAchren rode the raft to safety downstream and lived to celebrate the ride with Gertrude each year for the rest of his life.

Not everyone was as lucky as this, of course. The crest of the flood swept through Johnstown within about ten minutes and more than 1,000 people died in its first rush. Many others managed to ride rafts through the worst of the crushing water, only to die downstream in an unexpected fire.

Just below where the Little Conemaugh River and Stony Creek join is a high bridge made of stone. It had been built by the Pennsylvania Railroad and carried four tracks across the river valley. It had been built solidly and even the smash of the rushing tons of water could not shake it. At first the water flowed under the bridge. But soon the thousands of bits of debris began to hang on the supports. Within a few minutes, a huge jam of ruined houses, trees, and telegraph poles blocked the passageway under the bridge. The mound grew rapidly until it was 30 feet high in some places and a new dam was formed. Behind it, a large lake grew and the current slowed. Because of this, the damage below Johnstown was slight.

Hundreds of people rode the current into the jam of debris at the bridge. Those who could then scrambled to safety. But many others were trapped in their collapsed houses.

No one knows how the fire started. Perhaps an overturned stove was carried into the mass of timber in a crushed house. But it seemed to start in several places at once, just as the sun dropped behind the surrounding hills. Oil from an overturned tank car washed into the debris and the fire spread rapidly. Those people who had escaped the flood waters by moving to high ground were drawn by the flames that leaped upward in the darkness. As they neared the wreckage piled against the bridge, they heard the cries of the trapped people.

Without direction or organization, they swarmed over the tangled mass of wood and steel. At least 200 people were pulled from the debris by the light of the rapidly spreading flames. No one can guess how many others burned to death before they could be found.

The next morning was clear and bright. The water in the streets was dropping quickly. The fires at the railroad bridge and in a few of the nearby buildings were slowly burning themselves out. The terrible job of searching out the dead and cleaning out the ruined towns began.

A few more survivors were found in the debris. Some were dug from under the rubble near the edges of the jam at the bridge where the fire had not reached. Others were found in the ruins of their homes. One five-month-old baby was found nearly a hundred miles downstream at Pittsburgh, floating on the floor of a wrecked house.

But mostly it was the dead that they found. Hundreds of bodies were found, buried in the mud, floating in the water, and under crushed buildings. Other bodies floated in the water of the river and littered its banks for miles downstream. Nearly 1,000 of the missing were never found, and hundreds of the bodies that were found had to be buried before they could be identified. All in all, more than 2,200 people lost their lives in the catastrophe.

Without food, clothing, or shelter the survivors

of the flood were in a serious position. The threat of disease hung over the valley. The injured needed medical help. Nearly two hundred children had been orphaned and had to be cared for. It seemed to these people who had managed to live through the disaster that they were cut off from the outside world.

But word of the destruction of Johnstown reached Pittsburgh quickly. An official of the Pennsylvania Railroad organized a meeting of the city's businessmen into the Pittsburgh Citizen's Relief Committee. Within 24 hours after the dam had collapsed a train loaded with doctors, police, coffins, food, clothing, and medical supplies left for Johnstown. Six hours later, the train stopped at a section of washed-out track a few miles down the valley from the stricken town. By dawn the next day, June 2, relief supplies were being distributed to the survivors.

More help quickly followed. Among the hundreds of people who answered the call for help was Clara Barton, one of the founders of the American Red Cross. Although she was then 68 years old, "the Angel of the Civil War Battlefields" worked almost without sleep for five long months, distributing a half-million dollars' worth of money and materials. She also supervised the building of three large buildings to give shelter to the homeless.

During that long summer, contributions poured into Johnstown from all over the world. Three million dollars in cash was donated to the various committees that were organized to help in rebuilding the nearly destroyed town. Using dynamite, fire, axes, and shovels, the debris was slowly cleared away. Even more slowly the tents and temporary buildings were replaced by more permanent buildings.

Johnstown rebuilt itself and prospered as new industries moved into the valley. Many more floods have struck the city since that terrible day in 1889. Today modern flood control programs prevent all but the most serious floods from entering the city, but the people there still talk of the "day the dam burst."

CHAPTER THREE

FLORENCE, ITALY NOVEMBER 3-4, 1966

ROMILDO CESARONI looked at the rising waters of the Arno River and wondered if he should give a warning to the owners of the shops along the bridge. He was a night watchman and one of his jobs was to check these shops each night. After looking each place over, he would slip a piece of paper under the door so the owner would know the next day that he had been on duty.

He was an elderly man, but the work was not hard. In fact, ordinarily it was rather pleasant, riding his bicycle around this lovely old city while he went from shop to shop. Tonight, however, was not pleasant. It was raining very heavily, and it was cold. In fact, all during October it had rained almost constantly. November 1 and 2 had been bright and clear, giving hope that the rains were over for a while, but today it had begun again. This time it was more than a steady downpour. It was coming down in torrents.

The hills that surrounded the three valleys whose waters emptied into the Arno could absorb no more water. As the Arno received more water than was usual, the water level rose.

The people that Cesaroni passed on the streets that night did not seem to mind the weather. They just pulled their raincoats around themselves more tightly and hitched their umbrellas a little closer to their heads. Tomorrow was a holiday and the streets were decked out in flags. The Italian tricolor of green, white, and red hung alongside the red Florentine lily on a field of white. These flags had been fluttering in a slight breeze yesterday, but today they hung limply—heavy with water. The holiday was the 48th anniversary of the Italian victory in the First World War. Tomorrow there would be a parade and speeches, but tonight people were at the theater, or attending parties, because they did not have to work the next day. The sky may have been gray and the flags soggy, but the spirits of the people who sloshed through the streets were gay and festive.

The people who lived in Florence had seen the Arno rise many times. Ordinarily it is nothing more than a small brown stream, but when the surrounding land receives more rain than usual, the water rises. Cesaroni worried a little about it tonight. The river had a history of flooding, sometimes very badly.

It had not always been that way. When the countryside had been settled by the Etruscans about 800–600 B.C., it had been a clear, clean navigable river the year round. The hills were then covered with pine trees, several kinds of oak, beech, and chestnut. Ancient Etruscan pottery is decorated with deer and bears, indicating there was an abundance of animal life in the area. Now there is little. In the Fourth Century B.C., Theophrastus mentioned in his writings that beech trees from Tuscany were of such excellent quality that the wood was used for construction of ships' keels. In 300 B.C. the forests were so dense that the Romans were afraid to invade the area because it gave the local people such good cover for ambush.

The Etruscans planted olive trees and grape vines. They terraced the hillsides and planted wheat and barley in the bottom lands. They mined the area for copper, tin, and zinc to make bronze for weapons and tools. It was rich country and they floated their goods to Pisa on the waters of the Arno.

But something happened to this life of abundance. The land became overpopulated and the people abused the land. They cut off more trees than were replaced. An epidemic of malaria struck the people when the disease was brought in by outsiders from Africa. The planting of the hillsides was neglected, and there was not enough plant life to hold the rain-washed soil in place. Muddy water ran down the hillsides, filling the bottoms of the rivers with soil and raising the water level of the streams and rivers. This caused the low-lying lands to flood, and more good topsoil was washed into the rivers.

By the 12th Century, when the first accurate records of the Arno's flooding were made, all this had taken place. The hills were almost bare of trees, and the Arno no longer was a full-flowing, year-around river. When this early flood of 1117 was described, the Arno only flowed during the rainy season. The Ponte Vecchio, then the only bridge over the Arno, was washed away that year. It was rebuilt, only to be washed away or at least severely damaged several times over the centuries.

One of the times it had to be rebuilt was after the disastrous flood of 1333 that took 300 lives and swept away not only the Ponte Vecchio but two other bridges that had been built. Giovanni Vilani, who lived through this flood, wrote: "Wherefore everyone was filled with great fear and all the church bells throughout the city were rung continuously as an invocation to heaven that the water rise no farther. And in the houses, they beat the kettles and brass basins, raising loud cries to God of *'misericordia, misericordia,'* while those in peril fled from roof to roof and house to house on improvised bridges. And so great was the human din and tumult that it almost drowned out the crash of the thunder."

In 1545, Leonardo da Vinci drew plans for an

intricate set of dams, lakes, and locks designed to prevent a recurrence of floods along the Arno. These were never put into effect. He wrote a nephew not to settle in the Santa Croce area of Florence because it was damp and the Arno often overflowed its banks, filling basements with water.

Since that time men have often mentioned the flooding of the Arno in their diaries and histories. Ferdinando Morozzi da Colle made a study of the Arno's floods between 1177 and 1761. During that 600 years, the Arno overflowed 54 times—with a major flood occurring on the average of every 26 years and a very severe flood every hundred years.

Even 450 years ago, writers were warning their fellowmen to be aware of what would happen to our countryside if we only cut trees from the hill-sides and make no effort to replant and replace what is taken. In August 1547, Bernardo Segni recorded a massive flooding of the Arno. He wrote, ". . . because very great numbers of trees had been cut down for timber . . . the soil was more easily loosened by water and carried down to silt up the bottoms of the rivers. In these ways, man had contributed to the disaster . . ." Thus, man's concern with preserving our natural resources is not a new subject.

The hills that surround Florence still barely support olives and grapes, with occasional patches of scrub brush. The clumps are lavender, myrtle, rosemary, and thyme—sweet smelling and lovely when they are flowering, but scarcely good ground cover. The soil is hard-packed clay, that is almost

cement-like, allowing rain water to flow quickly to
the river beds with little being held in the ground.
This hard pan makes natural seeding of plants almost impossible.

And so, on that wet night in November, 1966,
Cesaroni kept a wary eye on the river. He knew that
if he called his employers, most would say, "Cesaroni is getting overly cautious in his old age. The
river comes up often and nothing happens. He
worries too much." On the other hand, it was beginning to concern the old man. As the water got
up to about three feet below the bridge, he began
calling the shop owners. Some of the people who had
jewelry shops on the Ponte Vecchio (which means
"old bridge") came with suitcases and loaded them
with their most valuable goods and took them away.
Others paid no attention to Cesaroni's warnings
until it was too late for them to safely reach their
shops.

By the time Fausto Raiola and his wife got to
their shop on the bridge, the river just barely swept
under it. They could see furniture, oil barrels, and
giant trees tumbling in the waters. By 3 a.m., the
water carried automobiles that smashed into the
bridge, causing it to shudder.

The Arno was flooding the lower parts of the city
and underground transformers were shorting out,
causing residents to lose their electricity. Since 9
p.m., the river had risen 18 feet. Automobiles left
parked or abandoned in the streets were filled with
the muddy water and ignition systems shorted out,
causing horns to honk continuously.

It was an eerie, wailing sound and was accompanied by howling watch dogs who were trapped inside warehouse fences. The horns continued until the batteries wore out, and the dogs were only silenced by the waters that covered them. The shouts of human beings, who were cut off from the rest of the world and in danger of their lives, mingled with the rushing sounds of water traveling through the streets and pounding against buildings. This was punctuated occasionally by the muffled explosions of furnaces and boilers.

The water came up so quickly and with so much unconcern on the part of people who were used to minor floods that over a hundred thousand people in this city were stranded in the upper floors or on the roofs of buildings. Many poorer people who lived in basement quarters in the low areas lost everything they had. Water swept through furnace rooms and carried away with it fuel oil that added to the miseries of Florence as the greasy black muddy water crept up the walls, leaving a giant, black, bathtub ring on the walls when the waters finally started to recede. This oil that was meant to bring warmth to the citizens of Florence also left its mark on the paintings and books that had been the treasures of not just Florence, but of the whole world.

At Cascine park, the Mugnone overflowed its banks and began to inundate the race course. Two hundred and seventy racehorses were in danger of drowning. Stable boys, owners, and trainers worked for three hours to get the horses into vans and to higher ground. When the water became so deep they could no longer help the horses, there were seventy left to fend for themselves. After the water had subsided, 43 horses were found dead. It was feared that an epidemic would break out in the area and flame throwers were used to get rid of the carcasses.

At 5 a.m., the chief of police called the mayor, because he was worried that the Ponte Vecchio would be swept away. In 1944 the retreating Germans had dynamited the buildings at both ends of the bridge, which weakened its foundations. The mayor dressed and made his way to the bridge to find trees hitting the bridge like battering rams as they were carried by the swollen waters at speeds of 40 miles an hour.

In addition to lives and homes that were in danger, the art treasures that Florence was famous for were being ruined by the muddy, oily waters. Dwight D. Eisenhower, when he was an Army general, had cautioned his troops, "All of Florence is a work of art." It was difficult to believe that what had been saved from war was being ravaged by Nature. Elizabeth Barrett Browning had called the Arno, "This crystal arrow in the gentle sunset." No longer a crystal arrow, the Arno now was a cancer of mud and oil that invaded basements and lower floors of homes, businesses, churches, and libraries.

At the Uffizi art museum, Professor Baldini and a small group of employees worked all through the night, taking paintings out of a basement room where they had been stored for restoration. The paintings were carried to upper floors where it was hoped they would escape damage. There was not time to save all of them, and so difficult choices had to be made. Some of the paintings weighed several hundred pounds. But this sturdy group of people worked as long as it was safe for them to be in the basement.

This city, famous for its rich heritage of artists and works of art was the home of the poets Dante and Petrach. Galileo, who studied the motion that would eventually lead to Newton's law of gravity, saw from Florence for the first time (through a telescope) the moons of Jupiter and the Lunar landscape.

In the early morning hours, the wet, oil-laden malignancy spread into the low-lying Piazza Santa Croce and crept up to a height of 20 feet in the ancient church of Santa Croce, covering the tombs of Galileo, Michelangelo, Machiabelli, and Rossini. The brackish, sewer-smelling waters stained the gilded surface of Donatello's relief of the Annunciation. Next door, in the church museum, the famous 15-foot painted Crucifix by Giovanni Cimabue, father of western art, was destroyed inch by inch as the waters continued to climb. At the National Library, more than 300,000 volumes were soaked with mud, oil, and sewer water. Most of these old manuscripts were irreplaceable.

Even the steel, safe-deposit boxes in the banks offered no safekeeping, as one author found later when he went to the bank. Papers that represented 15 years of research on Michelangelo, which had been placed in the vaults for safekeeping four months earlier, were now just mud- and oil-soaked pulp.

As the daylight hours came upon the city, it was gray and raining still. Katherine Taylor, an American author who was in Florence at the time, recalls getting out of bed in her upper floor bedroom and groping for a lightswitch that would not yield light. When she looked out the window at the Arno she felt a strange, magnetic force that would not allow her to leave the sight below. Where in previous days she had seen a small stream bordered by grassy flatlands and had watched fishermen in waders going out to nearly midstream, she now saw twenty feet of snarling, brown water that carried old drums, huge trees, crates, a child's red ball, and the body of a dead cow. As she saw tangles of household furniture, she realized that everyone was not so secure as she was.

A newspaper editor, Franco Nencini, spent the night at his newspaper and watched their new presses buried in mud. Huge rolls of newsprint were carried out of the warehouse and deposited to "wallow" in the street. When it was light enough for him to see out, he saw buildings that had become islands cut off from neighbors. People stranded on tops of buildings shouted messages from rooftop to rooftop. By this time all phones were dead, and gas, electricity, and drinking water had been shut off.

Soon Nencini heard a helicopter overhead. Every five or six minutes another would come in and lift mudcaked, despairing people from their rooftops and carry them to safety. One old woman was not able to hold on for the trip from the roof to the plane and dropped to her death in the swirling waters below as her neighbors watched helplessly.

A cold wind came up and moved across the already shivering city. People were stricken with fear by what they knew and by rumors they heard. There were tales of people drowning in basements and tunnels and subways.

There were many true stories to be told after that night. A hospital had to evacuate some of its patients by boat and care for others by candle light and flashlight. In addition to the sick, they now had people who were hysterical at the prospects of the rising waters. At the hospital of San Giovanni di Dio the water spread into the generators, causing the place to become suddenly dark. The doctors and nurses moved desperately to get frightened and ill patients from the ground floor to the upper floors. Since there was no electricity to run an elevator, these patients had to be carried upstairs. All the while, the water was covering the hospital's food supply with oily mud. They were able to save ten chickens and 20 bottles of mineral water, and on this they fed the whole hospital until emergency food could be brought to them.

In a children's hospital that was also without electricity, there were about sixty babies in incubators. The parents of these endangered babies were frantic until someone managed to bring in generators that had been placed on a stand along the parade route to be displayed for the celebration.

At San Salvi mental hospital, medicines were ruined while patients were moved to upper floors of the hospital, and the staff had no sedatives to calm the frightened inmates there. Eventually two of the staff members managed to get to higher ground and arranged for a boat to bring in supplies.

As the waters subsided and editor Nencini left his newspaper building to try to make his way home, he was shocked by the hundreds of houses that were half buried in a sea of mud. Someone described it as looking like a lake bottom, "slimy and reeking, seemingly buried forever." Nencini passed a dead man buried in the mud, with only his oil-blackened arm sticking out from under an automobile. People were crowding around, trying to lift the car while a woman who feared it was her husband stood nearby, in tears.

With the going of the waters, the residents of Florence were left with rebuilding both a city and a way of life for many of them. Twenty-seven people died in Florence and 16 others in the outlying province. Five thousand families were left without a place to live. Six thousand of the 10,000 shops of artisans and small merchants were destroyed. The tradition of handicrafts in Florence began in the Middle Ages when artisans chose their places for their shops because they could use the water power from the river to turn the wheels and lathes they used. In this modern day when the artisan was struggling to compete with machine-made goods, it seemed a cruel blow to have his place of business, all his finished work, his raw materials, and his tools ruined. But he still had his hands and his skills and with these he went back to work, to build something from nothing.

It was estimated that the Arno dumped 500,000 *tons* of mud in the city, which would be one ton for each man, woman, and child living in the city.

As soon as it was possible for people to begin cleaning up the mess, they were in their lower floors, shoveling out the waist-high mud that covered their belongings, and trying to salvage whatever they could. Life was very difficult for families who had lost their shops and jobs and also all of the belongings in their homes. They needed money to start a new business, to buy clothing for their families and furniture for their homes, and a new automobile. The young Italian housewives remembered with grief the big chests of fine linens they had collected and embroidered before their marriage—all ruined. It was hard to decide where they should begin to rebuild their lives. It was discouraging to think about how long it would be before they would be able to live even in modest comfort again.

But money was not the only problem facing the people of Florence. All of the shops that had sold food no longer had any. There was no drinking water in the water lines. Sewer lines were stopped up. And there was the problem of disease. Fifteen hundred Italian soldiers and policemen as well as 1800 firemen were called upon to help clean up the mess and hand out food and water, and to give inoculations to people who stood in long lines for these life-giving commodities.

Bulldozers and steam shovels were brought in to shove the mountains of mud out of the streets and into the Arno to make way for more mountains of mud that were moved from the buildings and houses into the streets. People tugged at trees blocking streets and cars overturned in front of their doorways, as well as other kinds of debris left by the receding floodwaters. Shopkeepers who had had jewelry stores on the Ponte Vecchio knelt in the slime and mud, hoping to retrieve some of their goods so they would be able to set up shop again. Divers searched the bottom of the Arno, hoping to find safes that had been washed away from the nearby shops.

People who had small linen and clothing shops rinsed the mud from their goods and laid them out to dry, a pitiful sight to behold. Passersby stopped to help with whatever needed to be done.

All over the world, people showed compassion for the loss these people felt and soon gifts from England, Germany, Austria, and the Soviet Union began arriving. Scotland sent blankets, water pumps, and vaccine; the United States rushed in food, clothing, generators, and prefabricated houses. Dutch engineers brought water-decontamination equipment, and Israelis provided a Christmas vacation on kibbutzim in Israel for more than 100 homeless children.

But more than money and "things" was the gift from hundreds of foreign students, including some

Americans from the Florence branches of Stanford, Syracuse, and Florida State Universities. These blue-jean clad young people gave their time and energy to dig in the mud in the basement of the National Library, hunting for old and priceless manuscripts buried there. They came to be called the Blue Angels, because of their long hours of digging through mud and slime. Blue jeans soon became mud colored, and for two weeks these students and other volunteers passed slimey, dripping books and manuscripts in a human chain from basements to upper floors where they were carefully blotted with a special paper to absorb the moisture. Then the books were loaded into U.S. Army trucks and sent to tobacco-drying kilns in central Italy.

At the National Library, there are still muddy handprints to be seen along the walls of the stairwell, giving testimony to the many students who formed that human rescue line.

Gradually light, heat, and water were restored to Florence and the job of cleaning up the disaster was made easier. The students left after the Christmas vacation, with most of the mud gone from the streets and sidewalks, but with many people still without homes.

In the Santa Croce area, which is ancient, many of the buildings cannot be lived in again. The city made plans to tear down buildings that were not safe and had no historic significance. They made plans to strengthen and rebuild those that they wanted to keep. These would have new plumbing

The photograph at the upper right shows the Arno River flowing quietly under the Ponte Vecchio, Florence's oldest bridge. As unusually heavy rains filled the Arno's channel to overflowing, water flowed through the historic Italian city. The flood damaged or destroyed many invaluable records and art objects.

and heating installed in them. When all of this was done, Santa Croce would be in better shape than it was before the flood.

Those people who were able to get back into their houses found furnaces that were full of mud and beginning to rust. And it was winter time. Buildings that were seemingly sound were still surrounded by the wetness of Florence and this wetness was gradually absorbed by dry walls and floors above. The tiles in floors that had not been flooded would suddenly begin to buckle and develop little hills and valleys. Walls that were thought to be dry would grow patches of mold and mildew. And if the furnace was not working, it was impossible to dry out the house. Overnight, the plaster of ceilings would bulge and fall. Springs erupted in basements, giving a constant flow of water in places. For weeks, walking about the streets was hazardous because, although the streets had been cleared of the deepest mud, there still remained a thin, slippery glaze of slime.

Everywhere Florentines waited anxiously for summer to come—summer with its sunshine to dry up the wetness and provide warmth for the people who would not be able to repair or replace their furnaces that winter.

In the huge church of Santa Croce, flame throwers were directed at the walls to prevent more damage than had already taken place to the frescoes there. All of the paintings from the churches and from the Uffizi basement were moved to the Limonaia, which are large greenhouses. There, in the heated rooms, the paintings were dried before it could be determined whether or not they could be salvaged. Some paintings were made on wood which warped, making it impossible to save them.

As the people of Florence cleaned and rebuilt, many blamed the city officials because no warning was given to the people. Their reply was that it was difficult to know when the river became a threat to the city. Also, if they were to ring the church bells in warning, the people would only have taken it as a sign of celebration of the coming holiday.

Plans were suggested for more dams upriver but there was the problem of getting enough money to build them. In the end, Florence remained as she had been before the flood—a city built in the wrong place. Florence is in danger of new flooding at any time.

CHAPTER FOUR

VENICE -THE SINKING CITY

THE SAME RAINS that flooded Florence fell on Venice during early November of 1966. They worried Professor Giordani Soika. From his laboratory in the Museum of Natural History, the meteorologist carefully studied the data his instruments had gathered and recorded. Again and again he checked his figures, but they seemed clear enough. A full moon that would pull the highest tide of the month, a strong wind pushing wall after wall of roaring whitecaps up the Adriatic Sea and onto the seawalls that protect the city, a falling barometer, and now a steady downpour. Soika added them together and, with a heavy sigh, made his prediction.

"We are in for some very high water," he told his assistant. "Call the City officials on your list and I will try the radio station and the Head Watchman."

The uniformed watchmen strolled calmly through the evening, ringing their warning bells. With just as much calmness, the radio announcers reported Professor Soika's warning. Throughout Venice, a city built on islands, the people who heard these warnings remained calm, too. They lived just inches above the water and occasional washing of their streets and open squares (called *piazzas*) by high tides was nothing more than a minor inconvenience. To most Venetians, the periods of high water were a small price to pay for the privilege of living in this lovely city of canals and marble buildings.

But this was not to be a normal "high water." The high tide of the evening of November 3 poured into the famous Piazza San Marco, as fall and winter tides often did. In spite of Professor Soika's warnings, almost everyone expected that the early morning ebb tide would drain the Piazza by dawn.

But at 7:00 a.m. the ancient paving stones of the Piazza were still standing more than a foot under water. The rain was still coming steadily down, blown almost horizontally ahead of a gale from the south. Tons of water piled up against the natural off-shore sand bars and 13-foot-high seawalls that protect Venice's lagoon from the tides.

By mid-afternoon, the tides had washed across

the protective barriers, had torn out most of the granite stones of the seawall, and were smashing across the narrow lagoon. Some of these waves made their way directly into the city, rushing up the famous canals and into the historic buildings. Other waves missed the island-city only to smash into the mainland and bounce back, entering Venice from the land side. Soon huge waves were crossing and re-crossing the wide piazzas and breaking against the doors and columns of churches and museums that had withstood the sea for centuries.

At nightfall, the city of Venice was helpless. The water stood six and a half feet deep in the lower parts of the city. Electricity and telephones had failed long ago as had the heating systems of almost all of the houses. Then, as suddenly as it had begun, the flood was over. The tide turned and the wind died and within a few hours the water drained from the city's streets.

First by lantern light and later by the dim light of dawn, the people of Venice looked at the damage. Broken gondolas and other boats littered the piazzas. Garbage and sewage lay in piles along the edges of the streets. And inside the houses and buildings, everything that had stood on the lower floors was ruined. For the first time, everyone in Venice realized that the scientists had been telling them the truth—Venice was slowly sinking beneath the sea.

The sea had not always been the city's enemy. Indeed, for centuries the water upon which Venice was built had protected her and helped her people

These people, crossing the Piazza San Marco on a bridge, now realize that Venice is slowly sinking into the sea.

earn fabulous fortunes. It was because of the water that Venice had been able to earn the title of "the most beautiful city in the world."

There was no city of Venice before the sixth century A.D. The fact is that there was no need for such a city during the time that the Roman Empire was at its strongest. The Roman citizens who lived along the northern coastline of the Adriatic Sea were, for the most part, wealthy and well-educated. The power of Rome protected them for centuries from the wandering, warlike tribes from central Europe and Asia.

But by the year A.D. 452, the Roman Empire had begun to decay and the protection of the merchants of the Adriatic became impossible. The vicious Mongolian tribe called the Huns followed their leader Attila to the very gates of Rome. Unable to capture the capital city, they turned their swords on the helpless, wealthy villages to the north. Attila swore to his people that "the grass will never grow again where I have walked," and town after town was attacked and burned. Most of the people who had lived in more than 40 communities were either killed or made slaves by the invaders.

A few of the merchants who lived closest to the sea managed to escape Attila's armies. They fled toward the water that had provided them with food and trade for so many years. Leaving the mainland, they tried to find shelter on the long, low sand bars that formed a quiet lagoon, but found that these too were unsafe.

Within the lagoon itself stood a cluster of tiny islands. These mud flats were inhabited by a few fishermen who built nest-like homes in the reeds that grew in the shallow water. It was here that the refugees finally found safety, for the Huns were not seamen, and in the crude boats and rafts they tried to build they were no match for the more experienced boatmen.

After the Huns withdrew, the people tried to return to their ruined homes. But more invaders followed Attila, and it was necessary for the people to return time and time again to the mud flats. It was finally decided that they would stay in their safe haven and try to build a city there.

They soon discovered that beneath the mud was a layer of heavy clay. Into this clay were driven thousands of tree trunks. These piles were arranged in a spiral pattern with their tops just below the surface of the water. Huge stones were then placed on top of the wood, forming a solid foundation upon which buildings could be built.

Over the hundred years that followed the invasion of Attila the Hun, the city on the mud flats grew and prospered. The people used their knowledge of the sea to build profitable businesses in transportation of goods from one seaport to another. From their own city they sold fish and salt.

By the end of the Seventh Century the city that was now Venice was strong enough to stand alone against the world. In the year 697, Venice declared itself a republic and an elected government was set up.

St. Mark became the Patron Saint of the city on the basis of an interesting legend. This story says that Mark had once been marooned on one of the islands in the lagoon where Venice now stood. As he slept, waiting for the storm to die, the saint had a vision in which an angel prophesied that Mark would return to the island. But he eventually died and was entombed in the city of Alexandria.

But the people of Venice felt certain that St. Mark was destined to lie in their city. One night, nearly 800 years after his death, some Venetian traders slipped into the sepulcher in Alexandria and stole the remains of the saint. Covering the bones with cabbages and pig meat (which the Muslim guards thought to be unclean), they managed to smuggle the holy remains back to where they felt they belonged. Eventually a beautiful building, the Basilica of St. Mark, was built to hold the remains.

By the time the Holy Crusades began, late in the eleventh century, Venice had become one of the major cities of the world. Her navy and merchant fleets sailed to every part of the world and her traders worked in every country. The war with the Muslims provided the Venetians with an opportunity to become even richer and stronger.

Rather than enter into the battles directly, the government of Venice leased some of its vast navy to the crusading Christian armies. With each victory, Venice gained in money, loot, and in new trading centers. By the year 1200, Venice could claim that she controlled three-eighths of what had once been the Roman Empire—from England to Greece and Turkey. The city itself was magnificent. Hundreds of beautiful buildings of marble and gold were built. Pricelsss art treasures from all over the world decorated the walls of these buildings and the broad piazzas. Highly decorated gondolas were poled up and down more than 200 canals that separated the buildings like streets. It seemed the magnificence of Venice would continue forever.

For centuries, Venice controlled most of the trade goods that flowed into the Mediterranean from the east—from as far away as China and

India. But late in the Fifteenth Century two amazing voyages took place that were to set the stage for the destruction of the city. The first of these was the voyage of Christopher Columbus and the discovery of the New World. The second, and more important voyage was that of Vasco da Gama in 1498. The Portuguese navigator had sailed around the Cape of Good Hope, the southern tip of Africa, and made his way to India. Within a hundred years, the new trade route to the Orient allowed Portugal to steal control of this valuable source of goods from Venice.

As their income from trade dropped off, the Venetians looked for ways to increase their sea power. It seemed logical to them that it was necessary for Venice to have a good deep-water port. But by the mid-1500's the lagoon that stood between the city and the mainland was rapidly filling with silt, carried into the lagoon by two large rivers. The leaders of the city decided that the courses of the two rivers had to be changed in order to stop the siltation. This job was quickly done and the port was saved, but the destruction of beautiful Venice had begun.

What the leaders of Sixteenth Century Venice did not know was that their city was not supported by the mud flats alone. The mud rested on layers of clay, and this clay in turn was supported partly by layers of fresh water—water that had for centuries been supplied by the now-diverted rivers. As soon as the fresh water cushions were drained, Venice began to slowly sink into the sea.

During the early years of the 1800's, the streets and piazzas of Venice were covered with water only three or four times a year, and only rarely did these floods do any damage. The city settled so slowly that few people really believed that it was happening to them. Occasionally a large building would settle too much and collapse, as the bell tower of St. Mark's did in 1902.

But the scientists knew. Over and over they warned the government of Italy that Venice would be destroyed someday. But it wasn't until the terrible flood of 1966 that they were believed. It was only then that Professor Soika was allowed to set up a warning system that would spread word of a coming flood before it actually hit.

But warnings do not stop floods. In 1967 and again in 1968, the tides climbed into the houses of Venice seven times. In 1969, twenty serious floods occurred. The Educational, Scientific, and Cultural Organization of the United Nations warned that within 70 years Venice will be constantly under water.

Another danger to Venice, other than the rising water, is pollution. As the city sinks, sewage that was once carried safely out to sea collects in the lagoon and washes back into the city's canals. In addition, air pollution from nearby factories has poisoned the air. As a result, the priceless art treasures of the city are slowly being destroyed. Within 30 years, some experts claim, half of the paintings and statues that have made Venice so beautiful will be gone.

CHAPTER FIVE

THE KANSAS RIVER 1951

THE WEATHER ALONG THE GULF COAST had been un-
seasonably warm and damp during the last part of
May and through all of June, 1951. A huge mass of
humid, hot air pushed steadily inland from the
Gulf and flowed northward toward the center of
the country.

Far to the north, along the Canadian border, the
weather was just the opposite. Cold, dry air rushed
down from Alaska and Canada, pushed by a large
high pressure area that sat solidly over the eastern
Pacific Ocean. This cold air flowed steadily southward, also toward the center of the country.

These two air masses—the warm, damp one from the south and the cold, dry one from the north—met each other over central Kansas. The warm air, being lighter, was forced upward over the colder air. As it rose, the Gulf air cooled. This caused it to lose its moisture in the form of rain.

The frequent rains had slowed the making of the motion picture that was being made in Manhattan, Kansas. The movie was being taken by the U.S. State Department to be shown overseas. Its purpose was to show the people of thirty countries something about how Americans live. Manhattan, a town of 19,000 people, had been selected as being a typical American city. The movie showed happy people living in a quiet but busy town—people who were content with their lives alongside the beautiful Kansas River.

The rain fell onto the flat plains of Kansas daily for 53 days, from mid-May until the middle of July. Much of this rain fell into the basin that was drained by the wandering Kansas River, while the rest of it found its way into the Arkansas and Neosho Rivers.

By late May most of the smaller rivers in Kansas and northern Oklahoma were out of their banks. On May 22, a driving rain pelted the little city of Hays, Kansas, and 43 blocks of the town were soon covered by water from Big Creek. Big Creek flows into the Smoky Hill River just below Hays and, as the rain continued to fall, water from the Smoky Hill spilled over the banks and filled the natural flood plains that line the river's route. Farther north, the Solomon River also left its banks. This was above the point where the Solomon joins the Smoky Hill and Saline to form the Kansas River.

Throughout June the rain continued to fall and low-lying farmlands and cities throughout the state were almost constantly threatened by floods. By the end of the month, the entire area drained by the Kansas River was soaked by the rainfall. Scientists estimated that the soil in the area could safely hold only two more inches of rain. But much more than that small amount was to fall.

It began late in the afternoon on the 9th. Rain fell steadily until noon the next day, at which time it looked like there might be a break in the clouds. But by nightfall on the 10th a steady, heavy rain was again falling over the entire drainage basin of the Kansas. Between the afternoon of the 9th and midnight on the 13th, when the rain finally did stop, more than 16 inches had fallen at three separate recording stations in central Kansas. Perhaps an eighth of this water soaked into the soil. The rest ran immediately into the stream channels, from there into the larger rivers, and finally into the Kansas River. The smaller streams began to rise immediately. By the afternoon of July 11, all of the larger rivers were over their banks, and the highest flood crest that anyone in Kansas has ever seen moved down the Kansas River.

Manhattan, Kansas, sits along the banks of the Kansas River at the place where it is fed by the Big Blue River. As the level of the smaller river rose filling its narrow flood plain, the tumbling water

Topeka, Kansas, became a deserted lake
as the flood cut the city in
two, and 25,000 people were evacuated.

from the Kansas boiled into the streets so suddenly that businessmen in the downtown section had to be taken out by boats. Quickly more than half of the town was under five feet of water, telephones and electric power were out, and thousands of people were homeless. The crest of the flooding Kansas River passed the town during the night of July 12.

Around dawn of the next day the crest smashed through Topeka, the state capital. This crest was three-and-one half feet higher than the previous record flood that had struck the city in 1903. Bridges collapsed, one carrying ten train cars into the water. Topeka found itself cut in two. Before dawn, water flowed over the tops of the levees and flood walls, and 25,000 people had to be evacuated. Railyards, factories, and businesses were damaged or destroyed, and a large section of the city became a deserted lake.

As the crest moved downstream, more water was added to it from the tributaries. The flood poured across the Santa Fe tracks for 55 hours, trapping 337 people aboard the passenger train *El Capitan*. During the afternoon of the 13th the water cut through the center of Lawrence and rushed on toward the twin cities of Kansas City, Kansas, and

Kansas City, Missouri. The two cities stand next to each other on either side of the Kansas-Missouri border. Near the center of the two cities the Kansas River flows into the Missouri River.

Almost a million people lived in the area in 1951 split by the two rivers, and it was one of the country's most important industrial centers. Hundreds of manufacturing firms, stockyards, packing plants, railyards, flour mills, and grain elevators lined both banks of the Kansas River.

But all of this valuable property seemed safe from the water of the river. More than 40 years before, huge dikes had been built that had protected both cities from damage from flooding waters. The dikes had been built to protect the cities from water five feet deeper than the flood that had struck the area in 1903.

Friday the 13th, 1951, was to prove to be a bad luck day. Even before the flood struck Manhattan, 130 miles upstream, the Army Engineers realized that Kansas City was in for a bad time. They calculated that the amount of water being carried by the Kansas River was perhaps 50 percent more than the river had ever carried before. A hundred miles ahead of the crest the river was rising six inches every hour. Uprooted trees and the remains of smashed buildings began to float through the city, smashing themselves to bits on the piers of 19 bridges that crossed the Kansas River.

The dikes that had protected the cities for so long suddenly did not seem high enough or strong enough. They were made of dirt piled more than

35 feet high to form a long, continuous ridge along both banks of the river. Rock had been spread over the dirt to prevent erosion. On the Missouri side of the river an eight-foot-high wall of concrete, three feet thick, had been added to the top of the dike. Now hundreds of people rushed to the edge of the river to try to make the dikes stronger and higher. Tons of rock were dumped into places where the river seemed to be cutting the worst. Thousands of sandbags were filled and piled on the top of the dikes at the lowest points.

But the river continued to rise. Night fell and the tired workers struggled with the heavy sandbags, using only the light of truck and car headlights. A man staggered forward under the weight of a sandbag and stepped into running water. As he dropped the bag into place he felt the ground under his feet shift.

"The water's coming over the top!" he shouted.

"It's coming over here, too!" another voice said from farther downstream.

"Everybody off the dike! We've lost it." The word passed quickly up and down the line of working men.

"Run for the bluff! The whole dike is going to go!"

The spot was on a large curve of the river, which runs almost due south for a time and then forms a loop to flow north where it joins the Missouri River. Here, on the right-hand bank of the river, the water moved the fastest and did its most rapid cutting into the levee. At first the water seeped through the spaces between the sandbags. Then it began to flow in a sheet over the topmost bags. Suddenly a sandbag broke loose and was carried away by the rush of water. Once a break in the dike had been found, the torrent enlarged the hole and for a while it seemed as if the whole river had found a new channel through the levee and into the city. A wall of water rushed through the railyards that stood behind the levee, covering $50 million worth of locomotives, freight cars, and buildings with muddy, swirling water. Beyond the railyards, two thousand people gathered up what belongings they could carry and joined the men from the sandbagging crews in a wild race for the bluffs beyond the town.

Across the river, on the inside of the bend, factory whistles and police sirens began to wail at midnight. Parents awakened their children. The more valuable of their possessions were packed into cars and trucks. Soon twelve thousand people were moving toward the high ground that stood to the north.

Behind them the river rose steadily in spite of the fact that the dike across the river was broken. Shortly before dawn the water topped the dike on the north side of the river along a four-mile-long stretch. Soon the section of the city that had stood within the river's loop was a lake. Only the tops of buildings more than two stories tall were to be seen above the muddy water. Rescuers in boats made their way through the streets searching for people who had not left their homes in time. Six square miles of homes, grain elevators, and manufacturing plants were under as much as thirty feet of water.

Many of the old-timers were slow to leave their houses. Some of them had lived through the flood of 1903 and refused to believe that this flood could be any worse. Among those was Emile LaBorde and her husband. When the sirens wailed, she was busily baking a cherry pie, certain that the water would never reach their house. But it did, and the LaBordes moved to the second floor. From there they watched the water slowly climb the stairs toward them. It rose until it covered the first step. Then the second step disappeared in the muddy water. Then the third, and the fourth.

When the water covered the ninth step and was less than five feet below them, the LaBordes gave up. From a window they signaled a passing boat and were taken to safety.

Throughout Thursday, July 12, the stronger dike on the Missouri side of the river held. Beyond the high, thick concrete wall that had been built on top of the dirt levee lay the stockyards, factories, and homes of Kansas City, Missouri. Here, too, stood the Turkey Creek water plant that supplied more than half the drinking water for the citizens of the two cities.

All day Thursday the water in the streets of Kansas City, Kansas, grew deeper. Across the broad lake, the water climbed higher and then higher still against the concrete wall. At dawn on Friday the 13th, 500,000 cubic feet of water flowed into the Missouri River each second. Soon water began to

"Do we have to pay to park?"
these men ask from their boat
on a flooded Manhattan, Kansas, street.

flow over the storm wall and into Kansas City, Missouri. Water flooded into the pumping station; the pumps stopped, and drinking water quit flowing from the faucets in the higher parts of the cities. The thousands of refugees who had spent two nights without shelter were now without drinking water.

The workers in the stockyards quickly herded cattle and sheep into the overhead shoots that were used to move the animals from one section of the yards to the other. Many of the valuable animals were saved in this way, but an estimated 6,000 hogs and sheep died and were carried away by the flood water. Within two hours, the stockyards stood under ten feet of water and boats were being used to take the workers from second-story windows.

By this time the flood water had invaded the very center of the Missouri city. Currents in the ten-foot-deep water washed debris of all kinds through the streets. Dead animals, smashed houses, trees, telephone poles, and occasionally the body of a human being were all carried along together. From somewhere came a large, steel tank partly filled with diesel fuel. Slowly it twisted and turned in the current. Around a corner it spun, and moved like an ocean liner into Southwest Boulevard. The current carried it toward the center of the city.

People in cities all along the Kansas River, like Topeka, Kansas City, and Manhattan, found themselves helpless as 53 straight days of rain pushed the river over the levees and flood walls.

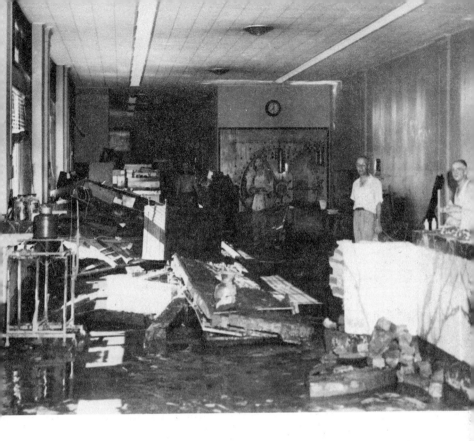

A few blocks farther on the diesel tank drifted into an area where two fuel companies stored their bulk fuel. The floating tank of diesel oil bobbed gently along between the building-sized tanks, each full of thousands of gallons of gasoline and other fuels. Suddenly there was an explosion. The drifting diesel tank had become entangled with a fallen electric wire. Sparks flew and the fuel oil caught fire with a roar. Burning diesel fuel spread quickly across the top of the water and was carried by the current from fuel tank to fuel tank. A tank containing 100,000 gallons of gasoline exploded, throwing burning fuel in all directions. Another tank of naphtha erupted like a volcano, adding more burning fuel to the water. Other tanks exploded quickly as the fire spead from one to the other in all directions. Within minutes, a quarter of a mile square sea of fire threw a single pillar of black smoke into the air.

Firemen worked from boats, pumping flood water onto the fire. But their efforts did little good and it was five days before the fire finally burned itself out. This one fire had destroyed ten million dollars' worth of fuel and gutted a seven-block area of the city.

The water flowed through the flooded cities and into the Missouri River. Downstream, the suburban city of North Kansas City began evacuation of as much valuable property as could be moved. Trucks and bulldozers worked steadily at shoring up the rapidly weakening levees. Hundreds of junked cars were thrown into the water in the hope that they would protect the levees from being eroded away.

But on Saturday morning water began seeping through the floodgates and under the dikes in both directions from where the Kansas River joins the Missouri. Finally, at 6 o'clock that evening, the dike collapsed and 20 feet of water flowed over four square miles of industries and homes.

On Sunday the waters began to drain from the streets of the two Kansas Cities and the people began the terrible task of rebuilding their homes. Throughout the area lay the wreckage of 2,500 homes that were totally destroyed. Sixteen million tons of silt and sand lay in the streets. Only one of the 13 railroad lines into the area was still in operation. Only two out of the 17 highways that once entered the two cities were still open. Seventeen major bridges had been washed away. And two million acres lay under the yellow water. Only ten percent of the area's sewers, water, and power systems were working. Nearly 500,000 people had been forced from their homes and had to be fed and clothed.

As the cities along the Kansas River counted their dead and began cleaning up the debris, the flood water rushed on into the Missouri River. Warned by the disaster upstream, the cities along the Missouri hurried to reinforce their levees. By the time it reached Jefferson City, the capital of the state of Missouri, the river had spread across the land until it was six miles wide. In this city, twenty blocks were swamped and electric power was shut down, but the main bridge over the river was saved when engineers piled nearly 100 tons of scrap metal on it.

Below Jefferson City, the story was nearly the same along the Missouri River. The citizens of every little town worked day and night filling sandbags and throwing them on top of the soggy levees. Trucks and bulldozers rushed to build new levees around water and electric power plants. Sometimes the dikes held but more often the levees crumbled and the water tumbled out of the river to spread over a million acres of rich farmland and into the homes of the people who had dared to live close to the river.

St. Louis, at the end of the Missouri, had nearly a week in which to prepare for the crest of the flood which had now reached a depth of more than 40 feet. A million dollars were spent on new dikes, sandbagging, and pumping low areas dry. As a result, the huge city suffered little damage. All of the bridges across the Missouri except one were closed for a time, a few waterfront buildings were flooded, and the sprawling railroad yards were awash for a few days. But for the most part the flood waters passed on into the Mississippi River without disturbing the people of St. Louis. The most costly flood in the history of the United States was over. Although the total damages to property was nearly $1,000,000,000, only 28 people had been killed by the flood.

Long before the crest of the flood poured into the mighty Mississippi, its victims upstream began the long process of rebuilding their lives. President Harry Truman, a native of nearby Independence, Missouri, toured the area and quickly signed a bill that would make $25 million in government funds available to the people living in the damaged area. Teams of men from the Army Corps of Engineers arrived almost immediately to begin rebuilding the levees that had been broken in hundreds of places. Inspectors and doctors from the Food and Drug Administration and from the Public Health Service moved into the area to do what was necessary to guard against disease. Flooded foods were checked for contamination and spoiling. Water purifying units were set up, and local waterworks were repaired and put back into operation. Refugee camps were set up in every available building.

In Manhattan, Kansas, the American Red Cross moved onto the campus of Kansas State College. Within a few days, one-tenth of the population of the city was living in the college gymnasium, the stadium, the field house, or the college hospital. Food, clothing, and bedding were made available to everyone. Drinking water was carefully boiled and everyone received typhoid shots to ward off the epidemic that might follow the destruction of the city's water system.

Before the flood, the town had a strong program of recreation. Realizing that the morale of the people would be very low after the waters drained away and the terrible damage of the flood was finally realized, the director of recreation for the city called upon his staff to continue their work. Movies were flown in from nearby Wichita. Museums and libraries were reopened quickly. Volunteers directed playgrounds that were opened on the lawns of the college and helped children to forget the terrible days and nights that had just passed. Comic books, horseshoes, and basketballs were shipped into the town along with medicines and food. Many adults, some of them wearing borrowed clothing and many of whom had lost everything they owned, soon joined in the nightly square dances that were held on the college's tennis courts.

The recreation departments of the two Kansas cities also did their best to improve the spirits of the flood's victims. It was felt that in addition to the medical attention, food, clothing, and shelter that were needed by those who had been in the flood, the recreation programs were also needed. Children needed to be cared for and entertained while their parents worked to rebuild their homes. Adults also found that they needed to have their minds directed away from the terrible damages that they had suffered. Other adults found that they could be of some help to those who had been more badly damaged by the flood through working with the children and older people. Through a well-structured recreation program, the process of rebuilding the lives of the flood victims was made easier.

The larger industries, because of their tremendous resources, recovered quickly. Within a few days or weeks, most businesses were in operation again and their workers were being paid steady salaries. But the small businesses and individuals recovered more slowly. Farmers found their fields covered by several feet of sand and had to plow deeply in order to bring top soil to the surface again. Small shop owners found their stock destroyed and their buildings badly damaged.

But eventually almost everyone did manage to recover from the damage and return to a normal life. The scars of the greatest flood the Central Plains has ever seen are now healed and life goes on. But when the rains begin to fall and the rivers rise, the oldtimers look at the new levees that protect their homes and remember the terrible floods of 1951. Someday, they know, history will repeat itself and water will again flow through their homes.

THE MIGHTY MISSISSIPPI

THE MAN STOOD ON A HIGH CLIFF overlooking the flooded Mississippi River. Under the black raincoat that protected him from the steadily falling rain he wore the brown work clothing and high, brown leather boots that were almost like a uniform to men in his profession. The man was an engineer. His name was Herbert Hoover.

The year was 1927 and Hoover was about to begin a job that was to help him become President of the United States in just two more years. But as he stood on the cliff top near Memphis, Tennessee, he was not thinking of the Presidency. He was thinking of the river below him.

In northern Minnesota, near the Canadian border, lies a lake named Itasca. From its northern end flows a little stream that grows into a wide river as it winds its way some 2350 miles southward to the Gulf of Mexico. This is the Mighty Mississippi River—one of the longest river systems in the world.

As the water from Lake Itasca flows toward the south it is joined by more than 250 tributaries. Water from nearly one and a quarter million square miles—about one-third of the area of the United States—flows through these streams and rivers into the river known all over the world as "Old Man River."

Water that falls on the land of northern Montana finds its way into the Yellowstone and Missouri Rivers and through these into the Mississippi. The Platte River carries water from Wyoming and Colorado to the Mississippi, while the Arkansas and Red Rivers drain the land of eastern Colorado and north-eastern New Mexico. To the east, the huge Ohio River Valley carries water that falls onto the mountains of Pennsylvania and West Virginia into the Mississippi. The southern part of the Appalachian Mountains are drained by the Tennessee River.

At its mouth, the Mississippi has built a huge delta of the mud and gravel that were carried along by the water from the land to the north. Upon reaching the delta, the river splits into many smaller streams, called distributaries. Through these, an average of 600,000 cubic feet of water is carried into the Gulf each second. But at times of heavy rainfall or rapidly melting snow anywhere in its huge drainage system, the Mississippi may carry four times this much water—nearly two and a half million cubic feet of water each second!

The mighty river has always flooded. Legends of Indian tribes living in the valley before Columbus' discovery of America tell of tremendous floods that uprooted the largest trees and carried away whole villages. The first European to see such a flood was Hernando de Soto, the Spanish explorer. For several years, de Soto and his men wandered through the river valley, in search of gold and silver. During March of 1543, the explorers were stranded on a cliff top for several weeks when the river suddenly left its banks and flooded the land in all directions. Later, when de Soto died of a fever, his men buried him in the river to protect his body from the Indians whom he had robbed and murdered.

In spite of constantly threatening to flood, the Mississippi has always been a valuable resource. Indians, explorers, traders, and settlers used the broad water as a "highway" for many different types of boats. Early farmers discovered that the overflowing water left tons of rich soil behind when it drained back into the river's channel. So, from the time of the first settlers, people tried to build their villages and cities along the sides of the river, even though they knew that every few years the river would leave its banks and threaten them.

The flood of 1927 was one of the worst in the long history of the river. It also proved to be one of

the most important, because Herbert Hoover was
there. During the next few months, he was to learn
enough about the problems of the river to make
many suggestions that would eventually help control such terrible floods as the one he watched from
the banks near Memphis.

Hoover had been born in Iowa nearly 53 years
before, and had been orphaned at the age of nine.
He had worked his way through engineering
school in California and then went into the mining
business. By the time World War I began in 1914,
Hoover had become a millionaire and was living in
England.

Hoover was a Quaker and did not believe in war.
So he immediately began trying to help the victims
of the conflict. First, he organized a committee that
helped 120,000 Americans, who had been caught
in Europe and England by the outbreak of fighting,
to get home. Then he organized a group to collect
and send food to Belgium, a country that had been
conquered by the Germans. When America entered the war in 1917, President Wilson asked
Hoover to organize the production and distribu-
tion of food in the United States.

He did these jobs well and many people suggested that he run for President in 1919, but he
insisted that he was not interested. Two years later,
President Harding appointed Hoover Secretary of
Commerce. He kept this job under President
Coolidge, and this was why he spent the spring of
1927 fighting the Mighty Mississippi.

The problems had really begun during the last

few months of 1926. During September and October, a steady rain beat down over the Ohio River Valley. Large rivers such as the Wabash and the Illinois were out of their banks much of the rest of the year, and the ground in the area was thoroughly soaked. The rains seemed to move southward and the Kanawha River of West Virginia overflowed during November. By the end of the year, major floods were smashing through the low lands around the banks of the Cumberland and Tennessee Rivers. In Nashville, Tennessee, 5,000 people spent Christmas mopping water from their homes.

As 1927 began, still more rain fell. It seemed that rivers in every part of the country were out of their banks. And the water that fell onto the central third of the continent all drained into one river—the Mississippi.

By the end of March the lower parts of the river were out of their banks and showed no evidence of returning to the river's channel. Then, as often happens during the early spring, a cold, dry mass of air from the north drifted southward until it smashed into a warm, wet mass of air from the Gulf of Mexico. The result was a rainstorm that dumped between 12 and 24 inches of water onto large areas of Oklahoma, Missouri, and Tennessee.

Rushing over the surface of the saturated land and into the Arkansas, the Red, the Missouri, and the Tennessee Rivers, these tons of water were added to the already overflowing Mississippi. Eighteen million acres of land were quickly covered by the muddy water and more than 300 people were lost.

At this time in the development of the United States, the Federal Government had no program for helping in the relief work after a disaster such as this one. But faced with nearly $300 million in damages, the Governors of six states called on Washington for help. In response, President Coolidge sent Secretary of Commerce Hoover with orders to do what he could.

Hoover had no money to work with at first, but he could call upon other Government agencies, such as the Army, the Navy, the Coast Guard, and the Weather Bureau. He quickly organized these into an efficient relief team.

Setting up his headquarters in Memphis, Hoover and his engineers found that the crest of the flood was traveling at the slow rate of only about 20 miles a day. Within a few days, the team of rescuers was working along the flooded river banks ahead of the crest.

In order to do this, Hoover needed money. But, as he later wrote, "At this time we all believed in self-help. Those were the days when citizens expected to take care of one another in time of disaster and it had not occurred to them that the Federal Government should do it."

So Hoover's first job was to raise money through contributions. A Red Cross drive by radio brought in $15 million. Another million dollars came from the Rockefeller Foundation. And $10 million worth of loans at low interest rates were supplied by the Chamber of Commerce. The railroads provided trains to help carry Hoover and his staff around the disaster area, and river boats of all sizes were loaned to him. Sawmills up and down the river went to work and made 1,000 boats in 10 days.

Coast Guardsmen manned the larger steamers and directed a whole navy of smaller motor boats in the rescue of people from the water that now spread out as much as 75 miles on each side of the river's channel. Navy planes circled the area, searching for people stranded by the high water. Engineers studied the pattern of the rising water and were able to warn communities hours ahead of the crest. After Hoover and his team got to work, only three people were killed by the flood.

Not everyone listened to the man from Washington, of course. Sam Dodge was one of these. He had lived alongside the Mississippi all his life. He had been born in the unpainted, two-story house that stood on a rise nearly a mile from the river bank, and in all those years the flood water had never come even close to the front porch. So Sam decided that the "big-city Easterners" didn't know what they were talking about.

Sam sat on the edge of his porch and watched the water come. It rose slowly, as it always did, covering first the low, black field where he usually planted peanuts. The water was red and swirled around the fence posts without disturbing them.

The next morning the peanut field was covered and the edge of the water had passed the row of trees that marked the dirt road that led to town. Sam tried to remember the times that the Mississippi had crossed the road. It had happened in the spring of the year he had been born—1883. And again when he was about five years old. All together Sam could count ten times in the last 44 years that the Mississippi had been this high, and he could remember stories that his father had told him of at least a half a dozen other floods. Sam knew, in spite of what that man Hoover said, that this flood would be like all the rest. The water would cross the road, brush the bottom of the hill, and then, within a few days, would slowly withdraw to its normal course, leaving a layer of rich soil over his lower fields. This deposit of river silt was what made Sam's farm so rich, and the flooding of the huge river was therefore a friendly thing—not something to be afraid of.

As Sam went to bed that night, the muddy water began to lap at the bottom of the hill upon which his house stood. At about two in the morning, Sam was awakened by a noise of some kind—a bumping sound. He lay in bed listening for a few minutes and then sat up and reached for the kerosine lantern that always stood on the floor near the bed. Muttering to himself, he lit the lantern and stumbled through the dark house and onto the front porch. The soft bumping seemed to come from under the porch, and Sam figured that an animal of some kind was there. Carefully he stepped from the porch—and found himself in cold water deeper than his ankles.

Startled, he jumped back to the safety of the porch. In the light of the lantern he looked out. He could see nothing but dark, swirling water and as he watched, it slowly climbed over the bottom step toward him. The flooded Mississippi was at least five feet deeper than he had ever seen it before. The Government men had been right after all!

Sam spent the rest of the night working hard. He carefully went through the lower floor of the house, looking at the things he owned and deciding which of them he wanted to save. These he carefully carried to the second floor. Later, as the water flowed through the house, he again carried all of his most valued possessions to the attic.

At dawn, the attic of the Dodge house stood like an island in the red current. Sam climbed from a window ledge onto the roof and looked around. For miles in all directions nothing familiar was to be seen. A few trees poked their heads above the water and away off in the distance he could see the tops of other buildings. The swirling, tumbling water seemed to cover the whole world.

The only noise that he could hear was the soft sound of water lapping against the sides of the house beneath him. It had now reached the second floor and was slowly rising upward. Then Sam heard another noise. It was a steady hum that grew louder and louder until it became the roar of a small airplane. Shielding his eyes from the early morning sun, Sam looked until he saw the plane, circling above him. He waved and yelled until the pilot saw him. The plane then dived toward him, flew directly overhead, and wobbled back and forth to let the stranded man know that he had been seen.

Back on the ground, the pilot of the Navy plane told his Commander about Sam's situation. The word was passed on to the Coast Guard squad that manned one of the steamers stationed nearby. Within a few hours, a small motorboat was on its way to rescue the farmer.

Once he was picked up, Sam was taken to the nearest camp. There he found a whole town of tents, pitched on high ground, far from the water. He was given a handful of tickets. He traded one of these for a space in a tent. Another was handed in for a bed roll. A third was used to "buy" a hot meal. Others allowed him to receive several shots to protect him from the various diseases that often spread through crowded camps for refugees.

At first, Sam was happy. He had escaped from the worst flood in the history of the Mississippi Valley and he had a warm place to stay. But soon he began to worry about his belongings. Would the flood water continue to rise until his house was covered? If it did, the things he had carefully collected over the years and lovingly carried into the attic would be ruined. The more he thought about this, the more worried he became.

Finally, the nagging worry became too much for him. Early the next morning he slipped from the camp and found his way to the water's edge. Searching among the trees, he finally found a small boat. He climbed in and began to row toward home.

After several hours of rowing, he finally found his house. The water had reached the lower sills of the windows of the second floor, but from the outside it looked to Sam as if the water had done little damage to the building. Getting into the attic proved to be quite a problem, however. Sam paddled around and around the house before he decided that he would have to climb in through a window and wade to the attic stairs. There was no way for him to tie the boat to the house so as he stepped to the window sill, he pushed the boat loose into the current and it drifted away.

He spent the afternoon inspecting the things in the attic. They were all undamaged and he settled down to sleep. The night was cold, and Sam was damp and uncomfortable. By morning he had decided that he would be better off back in the refugee camp. As the sun rose, he climbed back onto the roof and waited for another Navy airplane to cruise by. At around noon, one did and the rescue of Sam Dodge was repeated.

The Red Cross officials back in the camp were not very happy with Sam. But Sam was content. He felt certain that his property was safe from the flood waters, and he wandered around through the streets between the tents, talking with the other refugees. The only problem was that there was so little to do. Sam was a farmer. He was used to hard work. This standing around talking was boring.

Then the rumor began. Someone had heard one of the Coast Guardsmen tell one of the Red Cross people, the story went, that the water had begun to

rise again. The story wasn't true, but no one knew
that. Sam began to worry again.

The next morning, Sam again stole a boat. This
one had a motor and he got home quickly. He
found his house in good condition, considering
that the water now flowed in through the second-
story windows on one side and out the windows on
the other. He carefully tied the boat to the window
sill and spent the night sleeping among his favorite
things—the photographs and furniture that were
his ties with his dead family.

At dawn, Sam was stiff and cold. He was also
hungry. He decided that it was time to go back to
camp. He waded through the waist-high water to
the window and tugged at the rope. It gave so suddenly that he fell backward into the water. The boat
was gone! Apparently he had forgotten to tie the
other end of the rope to the boat!

Again Sam climbed to the roof of the house and
waited for a passing airplane. One soon came and
eventually a Coast Guard boat arrived to pick him
up. On board was a man in the uniform of an officer. Before the boat reached the house, Sam
could tell that the officer was angry.

"You're Sam Dodge?" the Coast Guardsman
asked.

Sam admitted that he was. If he had not had a tag
with his name on it tied to his shirt, he might have
tried to lie a little to this red-faced man in the
official-looking uniform.

"We are getting a little tired of coming out here
to pick you up, Mr. Dodge," the officer said.
"Three times is twice too many!"

Sam spent the rest of the trip looking at the water sloshing around in the bottom of the boat. He was too ashamed to look at any of the crew or at the officer. Once the boat had landed, the officer ordered Sam to follow him.

They walked a short distance to a railroad train and climbed into one of the cars. The inside had been fitted out as an office. A stocky, important-looking man dressed in brown work clothing and leather boots stood up as they entered.

"This is Mr. Herbert Hoover, the Secretary of Commerce," the officer told Sam. He then saluted the man behind the desk and said, "Here he is, Sir."

"Sit down, Mr. Dodge," Hoover said quietly, as the door shut behind the Coast Guard officer.

"You have caused us a lot of trouble, Mr. Dodge. The Coast Guardsmen tell me that they have made three trips out to your place to pick you up. Is that right?"

"Yes, Sir. I guess it is." Sam gulped and looked at the floor.

Hoover smiled and sat down in the chair next to the man. He looked him over carefully. This made Sam rather uncomfortable and he wished that he had a smoke. The man from Washington seemed to know what was going through Sam's mind, for he pulled a fat cigar from his pocket and handed it to the man.

"You are a farmer, Mr. Dodge?" Hoover asked. Sam nodded behind the cloud of cigar smoke.

"If it weren't for this flood, you would be plowing your fields now, I suppose?'

Sam nodded again.

"Living in the refugee camp makes you nervous, doesn't it?" Again Sam nodded agreement and puffed at his cigar.

"You would rather be working hard than just sitting around, wouldn't you, Mr. Dodge?"

"I sure would!" Sam said quickly. "You don't know how tired a man can get, just sitting around doin' nothin'."

"Yes I do, Sam," Hoover said, smiling. "A man who is used to hard work can get pretty bored with inactivity. But going back to your flooded farm isn't going to solve that problem for you. And everytime we have to send a boat out for you, we take a chance of not getting to someone else on time."

The two men sat quietly for a moment or two, one blowing little puffs of smoke toward the floor while the other sat watching him. Then an idea seemed to strike Hoover suddenly.

"I'll tell you what, Sam," he said. "Why don't you go to work for us. You are a strong man and we need strong men to work on the levees down river. We can't pay you anything, but it will give you something to do that will help save the farms of other people."

Sam quickly agreed and was soon on his way southward. Hoover chuckled as he carefully cleaned up the cigar ashes left by the farmer. One more problem out of the way for good, he thought. No one will have to rescue Sam Dodge a fourth time!

Some of the levees upon which Sam Dodge and hundreds of other men worked during the flood of

1927 were very old. They were made of earth and rock piled up in long, continuous ridges along the edges of the river's flood plain. The first levees in the Mississippi Valley were built in 1718, one year after the French settled in what is now the city of New Orleans. These early settlers found that their town was actually below the level of the water in the Mississippi and that any increase in the flow of water flooded their homes and shops. So an almost constant program of levee building was begun with money supplied by the French king.

By 1812, when Louisiana became a state, levees ran along the banks of the river for nearly 200 miles above the city of New Orleans. A huge flood in 1844, however, broke through these dams in many places and damaged many buildings. As a result of this flood, the United States Congress realized that local communities were not going to be able to control the floods of the Mississippi without help, and the first flood control legislation was passed.

By the time of the outbreak of the Civil War in 1861, levees had been built in almost solid lines from New Orleans to Memphis, Tennessee. But during the war the levees were neglected and some were damaged. As a result, floods in 1862 and 1865 caused much of the valuable farm land in the flood plain of the lower half of the river to be abandoned.

After the Civil War, money from the U. S. Government was again given to local communities to be used to build levees. But especially big floods still occasionally broke through the walls and some people began to suggest that the Federal Government had to take over the flood control problems of the Mississippi. But nothing had been done to put these suggestions into effect by the time of the flood in 1927.

Hoover and his men found the levees broken in hundreds of places all up and down the lower river. Working without a cent of Federal money, and without any legal control, they tried to convince people that they had to help themselves and each other. The 100,000 Cajun farmers of southern Louisiana proved to be the most difficult.

The Cajuns are the descendants of a group of French Canadian settlers. In 1604, the ancestors of these independent people settled in what is now Nova Scotia and spread into New Brunswick, Prince Edward Island, and parts of Quebec and Maine. They called their settlement Acadia.

As a result of the war between England and France for control of North America, Acadia was given to the English in 1713. During the French and Indian War of 1755, the English tried to make the Acadians take an oath of allegiance to the British king. Those who would not take this oath were deported, and sent south to the American colonies. Some of these refugees wandered into what is now Louisiana, where many French-speaking people lived, and settled down on small farms. They still speak a dialect of French and are known as Cajuns.

Hoover found these Cajun farmers to be almost as stubborn as Sam Dodge. He found it necessary to visit each of the little towns personally in order to convince the farmers that the flood was coming.

Hoover's engineers had carefully calculated how far the flood water would rise in one such town. Hoover arrived aboard his special train and called on the mayor of the community. The mayor seemed to be a highly intelligent man and quickly accepted the idea that his town was in real danger. But, he warned Hoover, the other villagers might not accept his word.

Hoover agreed to meet with a committee of the most influential people of the community. At the meeting, he explained that the water would enter the town on a certain day and that it would probably reach a certain depth. He suggested that everyone move their valuable possessions to the second floors of their buildings, build boats in which to move out of the area, and build a camp with lumber and tents that would arrive soon. He warned the people that they would have to be gone from their homes for about two months.

Everyone listened politely, and Hoover thought that he had convinced them. Then a man in the back row stood up.

"You are a Wall Streeter!" he shouted. "You are trying to get us to leave our homes so that you can rob us!

"I am the surveyor here," he continued. "My father was the surveyor before me. There never has been a flood here, and there never will be."

The audience muttered its approval of the surveyor's words. The Cajuns had lived here for nearly 150 years and they knew the river better than outsiders.

The mayor of the town was the only man in the room to believe Hoover. With the Secretary of Commerce, he visited other camps upstream and then returned to build his own.

Using materials supplied by Hoover and workers like Sam Dodge who came from the outside, he built a camp for 15,000 people and even built a cement wall around the electric power plant and connected it to the camp. With the work underway, Hoover ordered his train further south, telling his assistants, "A Cajun farmer won't move until the water reaches his bed!"

A few weeks later, the telephone in Hoover's train rang in the middle of the night. It was the Cajun mayor.

"The water is rushing through our town," he reported. "It started coming just when you said it would."

"Have you built your boats and moved everything upstairs?" Hoover asked.

"No, nothing but the camp is ready. The surveyor convinced everyone that nothing would happen. No boats have been built and nothing has been moved."

Hoover jumped from his bed and called to his assistants in the next car. Quickly they loaded a train of flat cars with boats. Not wanting to waste time waiting for the loading, Hoover ordered his train to head for the town.

Hoover's train arrived in town and found water standing ankle deep in the streets. The panic-stricken people stood helplessly in the quietly flowing current. Hoover assured them that the boats were following closely behind and that they would soon be safely taken to the camp that their mayor had built for them.

The boats arrived and Hoover supervised the loading of people into them. As soon as this job was done, he looked for the mayor. He found him wearing high rubber boots, sloshing through the ruins of his town with a huge grin on his face.

"Why so happy, Mayor?" Hoover asked.

"Some good comes out of everything," the mayor replied. "A few minutes ago the surveyor passed me in a motorboat, heading east, away from the camp. He shouted that he was leaving for good!"

A lot of good did come from the flood of 1927. Upon his return to Washington, Hoover reported to President Coolidge. He suggested that the Government needed to build higher levees along the river and along the tributaries. He also suggested that the Government should build a series of dams that could be opened to let flood waters flow into the Gulf through other rivers than the Mississippi, and a series of emergency storage basins along the main river and some of its tributaries. In the years since 1927, these and many other projects have been completed under the direction of the Federal Government and with Government money.

The world-wide depression that occurred during the years that Herbert Hoover was President of the United States slowed the work that he suggested. Therefore, the Mississippi Valley was not ready for a huge rush of water in the spring of 1937. The

partly completed levee system held and, while the
flood damage in the Ohio River Valley was the
greatest ever, flooding in the lower Mississippi Valley was fairly light.

By 1973 most of the work seemed to have been
completed, at a cost of about ten billion dollars. The
winter had been a bad one, with heavy snowstorms
that killed hundreds of head of cattle in the northern part of the Mississippi drainage system. As
spring came, so did the rain. Farmers in Wisconsin
fretted because they could not get into their soaked
fields to plant vegetables. The rain melted the
blanket of snow quickly and together, the melted
snow and the rain ran into the smaller streams and
pushed them out of their banks. Downstream, the
larger rivers began to swell. Still more rain fell over
all of the central part of the country.

By early April, most of the land near the river in
the upper part of the Valley was flooded—more
than seven million acres. But compared with the 18
million acres that had flooded in 1927, the damage
was not great. It seemed like the flood control
program of the Mississippi River was a huge success. More than 340 storage basins had been built,
as Hoover had suggested, and these were full of
water being held until it was safe to release it. A
flood gate was opened, allowing some of the extra
water to flow from the river into Lake Pontchar-
train and away from New Orleans. More than
1,300 miles of levees held the water to the channel
of the lower Mississippi. The water began to drain
from the fields and everyone began to relax.

But the rain continued to fall. Within three weeks, by early May, the water of the upper Mississippi drainage area was again filling the smaller streams and tributaries. At Keithsburg, Illinois, a levee broke and three feet of water rushed through the town. Around Quincy, Illinois, 4,000 people had to be moved from their homes as water topped the levees. In Missouri, dikes broke and 30,000 acres of farmland disappeared under the muddy water. Downstream people prayed that the levees would hold as more rain fell.

And, for the most part, the levees did hold. Weeks later the water drained away and the cost of the flood was counted. Nearly 35,000 people had been driven from their homes and 25 were missing. In all, 13 million acres of land had been covered by the water. Bad as this flood was, it was less than the damage done by the 1927 flood. One engineer estimated that without the levees, dams, and storage basins, the cost would have been seven billion dollars higher than it was. Hoover's plans for controlling the Mighty Mississippi had paid for themselves in one year.

CHAPTER SEVEN

THE "DEAD" HURRICANE CAMILLE, 1969

AUGUST 19, 1969, had been a beautiful day in central Virginia. A group of hikers reached the point where the Appalachian Trail leaves the Shenandoah National Park, paused for a cold drink at the restaurant on top of Afton Mountain, and then struck out along the more rugged section of the trail to the south. For ten miles or so this famous trail followed the top of the Blue Ridge Mountains closely. On the hikers' right lay the broad Shenandoah Valley. Through the many gaps and passes, the walkers could glimpse the city of Waynesboro, the shining blue of Sherando Lake, and the neat buildings and fields of the Mennonite farmers who lived simple, full lives along the steep slopes of the mountains.

The trail wound away from the road called the Blue Ridge Parkway and plunged off into the rugged hills that lie to the east of the Ridge. The hills were covered with dense forests of broad-leafed trees that were slowly shading out the pines that once covered the mountains. Springs bubbled out from under moss-covered rocks and tumbled downward through the trees. These tiny streams were joined, one by one, by other little brooks and the swiftly flowing water cascaded over dozens of magnificent waterfalls. These little mountain streams had names, of course, but none of these appeared on the maps carried by the hikers. Only the main rivers were named—the Rockfish, the Tye, the Piney. All of these eventually flowed into the mighty James River. This was Nelson County.

The 12,000 people who made Nelson County their home ignored the hikers as they did the rest of the world. They were more concerned about the ending of summer than they were about casual visitors who walked their mountain trails. They were not even very much concerned about the Democratic primary election that had been held that day to decide who would represent the party in the upcoming race for governor of Virginia. To them the golden hay in the fields, the apple trees on the high ground, and the haze that always stood over the Blue Ridge Mountains to the west were more important. In more than one house along the banks of the Rockfish River, peaches were being peeled and canned. On the banks of the James River, logs were being loaded into freight cars for shipment to the pulp mills. Along the Tye River, fence posts were being set and wire strung. Thick, yellow clouds of dust hung in the air over the Piney River, put there by the American Cyanamid plant. Elsewhere, men sat in the cool shade and talked of important things—like the time the revenue agent fell over the cliff and broke his leg while looking for an illegal still. As night fell, frogs began their songs from the quiet water of the many rivers and streams. Rain rattled against the window panes—gently at first and then more steadily. The late news on television told of Hurricane Camille and the disaster she had brought to the Mississippi coast a few nights before. But Mississippi was a long way to the south, and the people of Nelson County paid little attention.

Camille was the third hurricane of the 1969 tropical storm season. The storm started as a long, narrow area of low pressure that was first seen on a weather satellite photograph on August 5. The band of clouds drifted slowly westward from Dakar, West Africa, toward the Gulf of Mexico. On the morning of August 14, a Navy Hurricane Hunter plane flew through the storm near Grand Cayman Island and reported winds of nearly 60 miles an hour and a minimum air pressure of 999 mbs. Early the next morning, the winds topped 75 miles per hour and the storm was given the name Hurricane Camille.

As she moved into the Gulf of Mexico, the air pressure inside the storm dropped and the winds grew stronger. On the 15th she brushed the western tip of Cuba with winds of more than 100 miles per hour and air pressure of 970 mbs, and then began to curve slowly northward, toward the mouth of the Mississippi River. On August 17 the center of Camille was only 200 miles south-southwest of New Orleans. An Air Force plane flew into her and found winds of nearly 200 miles per hour and the lowest air pressure reading was 905 mbs. This is the second lowest air pressure on record in the United States.

People living along the Gulf Coast between Florida and New Orleans were warned. "Never before has a populated area been threatened by a storm as extremely dangerous as Camille," the Director of the National Hurricane Center told them. Two hundred thousand people boarded up their homes and businesses and began to move to higher ground.

Shortly after dark, the winds and rain of Hurricane Camille smashed across the beach near Bay St. Louis, Mississippi. In the little town of Pass Christian the electric power failed at 10:15 p.m. and a few minutes later a giant wave, as high as a three-story building, crashed across the sea wall. The Trinity Episcopal Church blew apart as a wind that must have been nearly 200 miles an hour struck the steeple. Modern buildings of brick, steel, and concrete collapsed as the wall of water struck them with the force of a million sledgehammers.

The storm moved on inland, leaving behind 137 dead and millions of dollars in damaged property. Around noon on August 18th the center of the storm stood over central Mississippi. Its winds had died and the rainfall had slowed, so the Weather Service scientists decided that Camille was no longer a hurricane. During the rest of that afternoon, they referred to her only as a tropical storm. As the low pressure area passed out of Mississippi and into western Tennessee, she was again re-named. From that time on, Camille was called only a tropical depression and everyone thought that she was dead.

The low pressure area that had been Hurricane Camille seemed harmless enough. During the next 24 hours it moved slowly, following a path across Tennessee into Kentucky. As night fell on August 19, a light rain was falling over a large area of eastern Kentucky and the mountain regions of Virginia.

The dead hurricane moved over the Appalachian Mountains and joined forces with a band of heavy rain that had moved into Virginia from the northwest. By ten o'clock in the evening, radar scanners showed a solid band of rain nearly 50 miles wide and running from Sulphur Springs, West Virginia to Fredericksburg, Virginia. Near its center lay the sleeping people of Nelson County.

As the mass of moist air moved into Virginia it was forced upward by the mountains. The tons of water vapor that Camille had gathered from the Gulf of Mexico cooled and condensed. The rainfall increased. Within the next few hours more than ten inches of water fell onto the western slopes of the Blue Ridge.

The rain front smashed its way over the Blue Ridge and onto Nelson County. During the hours of darkness, 12 to 14 inches of rain fell over almost all of the county, and near the center of this storm a record 28 inches fell in approximately eight hours. A half million *tons* of water fell that night, and most of it ran off into the James River.

The James River starts in the mountains near the Virginia border and runs through the central part of the state to the Chesapeake Bay. Hundreds of tributaries carry the water from over more than 10,000 square miles of land into it. The sudden fall of water onto this drainage region caused the rivers and streams to overflow suddenly and without warning. Homes built along what had always been quietly flowing streams were suddenly awash. Walls of water smashed through dozens of narrow valleys, carrying homes, barns, animals, and people with it. One river rose 27 feet during the night. Another crested at 35 feet above its normal level. At one time, the James River at Richmond was carrying 222,000 cubic feet of water past the capital city *each second*.

Only a few people saw this downpour and lived to tell about it. At nightfall the clouds had begun to pile up over the mountains. Many people were to recall later that they had been different clouds than they had ever seen before. Instead of pouring over the tops of the hills as clouds usually did, these seemed to roll together from all directions and come to a peak over the ridge that separates the Rockfish River valley from the Tye River valley.

The Tye is formed by two branches—the North and the South Forks. These in turn form from dozens of smaller creeks that spring from near the top of the Blue Ridge. These smaller streams must have flooded in a flash, almost as soon as the rain started. By the time the water rushed over Crabtree Falls, high on the Tye's South Fork, it was a torrent that smashed full-grown, living trees to the earth and swept away all evidence of the picnic area and parking lot below the falls.

Along the steep-sided slopes the soaked earth gave way with sudden roars like thunder. Tons of rock and dirt slid down the hillsides. Huge rocks, some larger than cars, were uncovered and then mined from the sides of the hills by the rushing water. Together with millions of smaller rocks, these rolled and tumbled into the Tye River valley.

This has all happened before, of course. Shafts sunk into the valley floor show that it is made up of layer upon layer of water-washed rocks, evidence of four or five tremendous floods of the past. But that was all before people moved into the valley and built their homes on the thin soil that covers the rocks. In the path of this particular torrent lay the villages of Tyro, Massies Mill, and Roseland.

In a house above Tyro slept a mother and father and their two teen-age daughters. The first any of them knew of the flood was the terrible feeling of their house lurching from its foundation and then

Rain falling onto the more than 10,000 square miles of land drained by the James River has always been a threat to Richmond, Virginia, as shown in this photograph taken in 1877.

rolling over and over. Apparently everyone was washed from the house with the first rush of water and found themselves tumbling through the darkness. A wave caught the youngest girl and threw her into the top of a tree where she clung for nearly 17 hours. The rest of the family was later found, all drowned.

The cluster of houses that formed the village of Tyro was smashed next. In one house, the water rose slowly enough so that two small children could be gathered up by their mother and father. As the water rose, they could feel the house begin to move. Then the boards of the house cracked and popped and water gushed up through the floor. The bed upon which they sat floated upward until it hit the ceiling and then the whole house tore apart. The two children were pulled from their parents' arms and carried away in the red water. Only the parents survived the night.

Only a church and two other small buildings on the riverside of the road through Massies Mill withstood the water's rush. One man later described his house going "like a paper bag busting." His wife and daughter disappeared along with the house and furniture while he clung to a tree a half a mile downstream.

Below Massies Mill, on a bend in the Tye, stood the few houses and the post office of Roseland. A huge landslide cascaded down the side of the mountain just above the village and, for a few minutes, blocked the flow of water down the Tye valley. The water above the dam continued to build up and then, suddenly, it broke through. A wall of water perhaps 25 feet high tore first through the opening and then through Roseland. The next day, rescue parties found only one house left, and it was turned on its side.

By the time the dam broke, debris from upstream had reached it. A lineman for the local electric company stood helplessly on the hillside and watched as pieces of houses and barns washed past in the light of his spotlight. Trucks, cars, and the bodies of cows and horses rushed past him. Soon people were seen, riding the ruins of their homes or clutching to the sides of bales of hay. One by one they would be caught as the current washed them through the narrow channel and then be overwhelmed by the water where the ruins of a smashed bridge caused the river to crest.

Across the ridge, along the drainage basin of the Rockfish River, the destruction was just as bad. The sun had set on 75 people living in 26 small houses and trailers along Davis Creek. Now an avalanche of water, mud, rocks, and tangled trees roared through the little community for nearly four hours. A huge landslide smashed down onto one home, burying nine people. The bodies of 40 others were carried away by the current to be left in the mud or hanging from broken trees farther downstream.

It rained on the west side of the Blue Ridge, too, but not as heavily as in Nelson County. Beyond the gap cut through the ridge by the James River stood the little industrial town of Buena Vista. By three in the morning of August 20 the Maury River had cut the city into three sections. Civil defense sirens wailed as a bridge gave way. Water flowed through 65 homes and flooded equipment and stocks of 87 businesses. Electric power failed and the sewage system was shut down as water flowed over it. In the town and surrounding countryside, 23 people drowned and the area suffered nearly $9 million in property damages.

Farther to the north along the western edge of the Blue Ridge the rain was much lighter. The South River quickly reached flood stage and flowed into the streets of Waynesboro. The fields along the river disappeared under the swirling current.

One of these farms was owned by a man named Jonas Kanagy. He is a short, stocky, powerful-looking man with the strong hands of a skilled craftsman, the deep voice of a leader, and the quick laugh of a man at peace with the world. A member of the Mennonite Church, he wears a wisp of grey-flecked beard, a blue workshirt, and black trousers. He is important to our story because he is the Unit Leader for the Mennonite Disaster Service that is centered in the Shenandoah Valley of Virginia.

The Mennonite Disaster Service was organized as a result of a picnic held on the prairies of Kansas. It developed because of the feeling of a group of young men that their church organization could be used to help their fellowmen. "We wish to follow Christ and His teaching in all our living," they said. "We consider anyone in need to be our neighbor."

That was in 1951. Since that time, the organization has grown until it covers all of the United

States and Canada, and reaches into Germany, Nicaragua, Haiti, Vietnam, and Bangla Desh. More than $16 million has been given by the Mennonite people to help the victims of disasters in these countries.

Kanagy got up early, as he always does, on the morning of August 20. Like all farmers of whatever faith, he first looked out to see what damage his fields had suffered from the moderately heavy rain of the night before. To his surprise he looked out onto a lake nearly a quarter of a mile across.

He found his road covered by more than a foot of water, so he headed across the higher fields in a borrowed Jeep. By using back roads and open fields, he finally made his way to the city of Waynesboro. There he found that no one had been drowned, although the lower streets were full of water. Rescue Squads from neighboring towns were already at work evacuating those people who had been trapped in their flooded homes. He was told that the Mennonites were not needed here today. But there were rumors that the damage down the valley had been worse than here in Waynesboro.

The further down the valley he drove, the more amazed he was at the damage. Huge trees and rocks lay in tangled piles everywhere. What were normally quiet little streams now covered roads and bridges with huge lakes of water. Houses stood at crazy angles where they had been knocked from their foundations or lay in splintered heaps. Everywhere roads were blocked by the water or by damaged bridges. He returned home that night without having gotten into the most damaged regions, but he was convinced that his area had been hit by a terrible disaster.

Normally, when a disaster strikes, a Mennonite in the area contacts the Region I Leader—the man in charge of the Mennonite Disaster Service works along the East Coast. He in turn calls the National Leader in Pennsylvania. From here, Unit Leaders are directed into the disaster area. Kanagy passed the word on to his Regional Leader, but, since he was in charge of the local unit, he went to work immediately without waiting for orders from the National Headquarters.

But he found that his local unit was not ready for a disaster. His telephone calls to the local Mennonite homes produced only a few volunteers. It was haying time and no one wanted to leave their own work. The unit was, as Kanagy later said, like a piece of farm machinery that had "rusted out from sitting in the shed too long." Somehow, he knew, the machine had to be "dragged out in the open and oiled up before it would run again."

By telephone he sent word out to the outer edges of his unit. Finally a group of Old Order Mennonites agreed to come. Discouraged with the attitude of his neighbors, Kanagy went to bed determined to work with the outside group as best he could.

By Saturday afternoon, nearly 36 hours after the flood, Kanagy managed to reach Buena Vista, which is normally less than an hour's drive from his home near Waynesboro. There he found more

Jonas Kanagy

than enough work for his people to do. Later an Army helicopter took him over the mountains and into Nelson County. For the first time he saw how great the damage really was.

Finally, the Red Cross called. "We need men," he was told. "We need a lot of men Monday morning."

Kanagy again began calling his neighbors. If they were not willing to work, would they take care of the outsiders who might come, he asked them. He found places to sleep 15 people.

Then more phone calls went out, this time to Pennsylvania and Maryland Unit Leaders. "I need 15 men," he told them. "I need a lot more, but that is all the room I can find."

Early Monday morning, Kanagy stood alongside his pickup truck in the parking lot of the Howard Johnson's Restaurant. In his mind, he planned out the day as best he could. He would take the 15 men from the Pennsylvania and Maryland Units into Buena Vista where he was to meet the Red Cross official. Hopefully, the men from the Red Cross would have work for them to do.

Somewhere in the back of his mind was the shadow of doubt. His own neighbors were still not volunteering to work, in spite of all the talking he had done after church the day before. He had told them how the other side of the mountain had looked from the air—about the huge landslides, the washed-out bridges, the tangles of uprooted trees, and the smashed houses. A few had finally agreed to give up a day or two from their farm work, but most of them felt that if they housed and fed the workers from the outside they would have done their part.

He also worried about the workers from the outside. The Unit Leaders that he had called had assured him that they could easily get 15 men to come down for a week. Kanagy knew that these units, unlike his own, had experienced many disasters in their areas and had the reputation for being ready to act. But he found himself breathing a sigh of relief as two cars with Pennsylvania licence plates pulled into the parking lot. Twelve men, each with nearly identical black, spade-shaped beards got out and walked toward him.

As they introduced themselves to the relieved

Kanagy another car from Pennsylvania arrived, followed by one with Maryland plates. Kanagy was overjoyed. Twenty-four instead of 15! He would have a little problem with finding a place for all of them to sleep, but at least the Mennonites were here and ready to help.

But as he started to give directions for the drive to Buena Vista, another Maryland car arrived. And then another. Then two more from Pennsylvania. More and more black-bearded men crowded into the parking lot. When the last car finally arrived, Kanagy's crew had grown to a total of 82 men!

Amazed, shocked, and very pleased, Kanagy climbed to the back of his truck and thanked the men for coming. "But," he explained, " we don't have room for all of you to spend the night."

"Find places for as many as you can," he was told. "The rest of us will drive back home each night."

"But that would be a three or four hour drive in the morning, a hard ten or twelve hours working here, and then another three or four hours' drive back home. That's a terribly hard day!"

"Not as hard a day as those people in the mountains are having. Let's go to work!"

But "going to work" wasn't quite as easy as it sounds. Kanagy did not know the area around Buena Vista very well and had no authority to act in the area at all. Before he and his fellow workers could do anything he first had to find someone who knew what needed to be done and who could get them through the police roadblocks that had been put up to keep out idle sightseers.

Normally, the Mennonite Disaster Service works very closely with the American Red Cross. The Red Cross has a supply of money ready to use in emergency situations and the organization has experienced case-workers who can identify the people who need help the most. But in this disaster, something went wrong. The Red Cross couldn't seem to get itself into action. When Kanagy and his men arrived in Buena Vista, no one was there to meet them.

Fortunately, the town of Buena Vista had an active Civil Defense organization, with very strong leadership. Within a few hours, the Mennonites were hard at work under the supervision of the Civil Defense Director.

That night, most of the men left for their own homes in Maryland and southern Pennsylvania. Kanagy gave directions to those men who were to spend the night with local Mennonite families. He explained how difficult it had been to get any help from the local people.

"They don't realize how bad it is," he said. "Don't wash up before you go in. Let them see how dirty you got today. Let them know how hard you worked. Tell them what we have to do."

That night the telephone at the Kanagy house rang almost all night. Word of the good work that had been done in Buena Vista that day had spread across the mountains and the Civil Defense organization in Nelson County called for help from the Mennonites. But most important to Kanagy, local Mennonites had also gotten the message he had

sent by way of the overnight guests. Volunteers
from the local group called in by the dozens.

The next day Mennonites began work in all parts
of the disaster area. By now everyone realized just
how big the area was. The storm had cut a path
through the mountains that was nearly 100 miles
long and 30 miles wide—3,000 square miles of
mud, smashed houses, and death. Kanagy's main
job was to find the jobs that needed his volunteers
the most.

The job that seemed to be the most important
was to find the bodies of the people killed in the
flood. The coordination of this work was the re-
sponsibility of the Civil Defense organizations in
the different communities. It was fortunate that
this important work fell to these organizations because they seemed to be the only people who were
really ready for the emergency. No one knew how
many bodies lay in the debris and mud of the 3,000
square mile area. The Civil Defense officers di-
vided their areas up among the groups of volunteers. The Mennonites were given three areas—
one near Buena Vista, another in Lovingston (the
Nelson County seat), and a third in the heart of the
Tye River Valley.

During the next two and a half weeks, Kanagy
and his group searched the wreckage for bodies.
Some were easily seen—lying in their smashed
homes, half buried in the mud, or hanging from
trees as much as 20 feet above the ground. As the
days wore on, the job became more difficult.

"You may have to use your sense of smell,"

Kanagy told his men. "And watch for signs that animals have found something—buzzards gathering over a certain spot or animal tracks leading toward a pile of debris."

It was hot in late August and the smell in the air along the Tye became more and more nauseating. Many groups helped with the dirty job of finding and digging out the decomposing bodies, but the Mennonites carried the major load. On Labor Day weekend, two full weeks after the flood, the final push to find the dead was started. Kanagy was asked to bring 35 men, and out went the call for volunteers. Of the 500 men who worked that weekend, 278 were Mennonites!

Nearly 200 bodies were eventually found, but two dozen people are still missing—probably buried under many feet of mud and sand in some now-quiet stream. Perhaps someday they will be found. Two men were found, in the spring of 1970, nearly seven months after the flood.

There were other jobs to be done in addition to the finding of bodies. Many of the homes that had not washed away were full of mud, left when the water drained away. This needed to be shoveled into buckets and carried away. And many of the homes were badly damaged and needed to be repaired or replaced.

Kanagy found that the people who had been hardest hit by the flood were confused and seemed to be unable to help themselves. He found them standing, staring at the ruins of their homes, remembering the members of their family that had suddenly been killed, unable to think about their future.

"They don't know what to do," Kanagy told his people. "They need someone to come in and say what needs to be done. As soon as we pick up a board or take out a bucket full of mud, they will start gathering up. They will blossom out, just like a plant in a rain after a long dry spell."

One church in the Tye Valley withstood the water but had 18 inches of mud covering its floor. Only three of the church's members showed up to help the 35 Mennonites who went in to clean up the mess. The Minister later said, "I used to believe that our people were the only ones who were going to heaven. Now I've changed my mind."

By this time the Red Cross had gotten itself organized and its case workers were finding jobs that the Mennonites could do. Kanagy sent out a call for skilled carpenters. Before it was over, they built 34 new homes and repaired 55 others. They also built 16 barns, one store, and six bridges. As the rocks were moved from the fields, the Mennonites planted grass and trees.

By the spring of 1970 the town of Buena Vista seemed to be on the road to recovery. Better organized and with more industry, the town became able to take care of itself more quickly than did neighboring Nelson County. So the Mennonites concentrated their efforts on the eastern slope of the mountains. It was Christmas, more than 16 months after the flood, before the black-bearded men finally packed up their tools and left the region. Kanagy estimates that the Mennonites donated a total of 20,000 man-days to helping the victims of the flood.

A drive through the Tye River Valley now shows you few scars of those terrible hours in 1969. The river tumbles quietly over rocks that are not worn smooth yet, and piles of broken rocks that were pushed from the fields still line the banks of the river. Roseland is not where the map says it should be—it now is a cluster of new homes standing high on a hill a mile or so north and high above the river. New homes, many of them built by the Mennonites, dot the valley. And the Mennonite grass and trees are growing well.

Over the mountains, Jonas Kanagy still spends most of his time doing relief work. He has sold his farm and makes enough money for his own needs by building houses. But often, if the house is to replace one lost by fire or some other disaster, he charges nothing.

"I can't charge these poor people who have suffered a loss," he says. "To the man whose house has burned down, it was just as big a disaster as if the whole county had been hit. We are here to help our neighbors—whether it's one family who happens to live next door or a whole country a thousand miles away."

Until 1969, the Mennonite Disaster Service would not take donations of money unless they could spend it all on the spot. But they learned that a disaster the size of the Virginia flood could put a terrible strain on their treasury. Donations are now taken whenever they are offered and, if not needed immediately, they are kept until another disaster strikes.

"We learned a lot during the 1969 flood," Kanagy told us. "We learned how to use radio communications and helicopters for the first time. And we learned that we need to be able to pay a leader to stay on the job until it is finished. We also learned that we need a strongly organized group on the outside backing up the relief work. '

"Back in 1964 I went with a group of Mennonites to Haiti after that country had been smashed by a hurricane. We were warned before we went that we might not survive. If we got put in jail, they told us, the Mennonite Disaster Service wasn't going to be able to get us out. In fact, since the government down there didn't feed its prisoners, it would be likely that we would starve to death if we got put in jail.

"Francois Duvalier was dictator then, and he was a terribly hard-hearted man. He had killed thousands of his own people trying to keep control of the country. But when we left, he gave us a citation and told us that the country was open to us any time we wanted to come back.

"Work like ours will move the hardest heart," he said, looking at his work-scarred hands. "You can subdue a people by force, but if you win them by love, you have *really* won. The best way to get rid of an enemy is to make a friend out of him.

"There is nothing stronger than genuine love, applied in a genuine way."

CHAPTER EIGHT

"THE PALM OF THE HAND OF GOD" (IMPERIAL VALLEY, CALIFORNIA)

THIS IS THE STORY of a very unusual flood. It lasted for two years, caused millions of dollars in damages, left behind a lake that can still be seen more than 70 years later, but killed no one. This is also the story of men who wanted to make the desert bloom, men who wanted to make money quickly and who didn't care about the welfare of anyone else, and about men who learned to control a huge river. But most of all, this is the story of a desert basin in southern California.

The low-lying desert area was called *La Palma De La Mano De Dios*—The Palm of the Hand of

God—by the Spanish-speaking people who lived nearby. Its history began many centuries ago. At least, the valley was formed long before anyone began keeping a history of the region that now lies on the border between California and Mexico.

Geologists, scientists who study the earth and its history, tell us that at one time the Gulf of California ran many miles much farther to the north than it now does. Near the northern end of the Gulf, the water must have stood nearly 300 feet deep. Into this large arm of the ocean flowed the river we now call the Colorado.

Rain that falls on parts of Wyoming, Colorado, Utah, New Mexico, Arizona, Nevada, and California finds its way to the sea through the Colorado River. The river also carries along with this water tons of silt and sand from the surface of the more than a quarter of a million square miles of land that it drains. This is the river that dug out the mile-deep Grand Canyon.

Centuries ago, as this rushing water entered the quiet water of the Gulf of California, it slowed and dropped the load of sediment it was carrying. Slowly this sand and silt accumulated until a huge delta was built at the mouth of the river. As more sediment flowed down from the mountains, the delta grew. Finally the delta became so large that it completely blocked the upper end of the Gulf.

To the north of the delta dam now stood a huge inland salt lake, completely cut off from the sea. The Colorado River found new paths to the Gulf across the delta and no water flowed into the new

salt lake. Eventually, over hundreds or perhaps
thousands of years, the water in the lake evaporated and left the basin exposed to the air.

This basin is over 200 miles long and nearly 50
miles wide, and more than one-fourth of it is below
sea level. Its lowest point is 273 feet below the level
of the water in the Gulf of California—almost as
low as the more famous Death Valley. To the early
Spanish explorers, it looked from the surrounding
hills like the depression in an open hand. So, they
named it "La Palma De La Mano De Dios."

At first, the early American settlers avoided the
basin, which they called the Salton Sink. The men
who rushed to California to look for gold in 1849
found it a place to cross quickly on their way to
more pleasant surroundings. In the summer, the
temperature in the Sink often reached 125 degrees,
and in an average year only three inches of rain
fell. To the south and east, between the basin and
the Colorado River, stretched an area of sand
dunes that were all but impossible to cross on foot
or horseback. Beyond the San Bernardino Mountains to the north lay the Mojave desert and Death
Valley. Westward, across the crinkly San Jacinto
and Laguna Mountains, was San Diego and the
Pacific Ocean. In the last years of the 19th century,
as California's population grew toward a million,
no one lived in the Salton Sink. Then, shortly before 1900, two men came to the desert basin, one
with a dream, the other with money and technical
knowledge.

The first man was Charles Rockwood, a young

engineer and surveyor. His idea was to use the water of the Colorado River to irrigate the rich-but-dry soil of the Sink. He realized that the river was higher than most of the bottom of the basin and believed that a canal could be dug that would allow water to flow downhill into the Sink. It was a good idea and he knew it would work, but he needed money and someone who understood irrigation work.

George Chaffey met both of these requirements. He had just completed a huge irrigation project near Los Angeles and was looking for a place to invest the money he had made and a job that needed his talents. For six weeks the two engineers surveyed the basin and the land around it.

Chaffey liked what he saw. The soil of the Sink was fertile, except for those places that had been spoiled by the salt left when the sea water evaporated. The basin was normally free from frost for more than ten months each year and farmers would be able to get two crops each year under the burning summer sun. Rain fell so rarely that it would never interfere with harvests. And the tracks of the Southern Pacific Railroad passed nearby, so trains would be able to rush fresh fruits and vegetables to New Orleans quickly.

The only real problem seemed to be the digging of the canal. It would be impossible, Chaffey knew, to dig a ditch through the sand dunes that lay between the river and the Sink with the equipment then available. He searched carefully through the dunes until he found a dry riverbed that ran across the delta from Mexico nearly to the entrance of the Sink. The riverbed was full of loose silt and sand and this should have warned Chaffey that the Colorado River had overflowed and used the old river as a drainage canal sometime in the past. But the engineer was anxious to see the project move forward, and he overlooked this evidence.

In November, 1900, work was begun on a stretch of canal that would carry water from the Colorado to the dry riverbed in Mexico. The amount of water that could flow into the canal would be controlled by a huge concrete flood gate. After passing the gate, which stood across the river from Yuma, Arizona, the water would flow toward the south alongside the main channel of the river. Several miles inside Mexico, Chaffey's canal would meet the dry riverbed and the water would flow north again. Short, feeder canals were designed to distribute the water to farms scattered throughout the valley.

Advertisements were sent out all over the country telling people that the valley would soon be ready for farming. But Chaffey was too smart to try to get people to move to a place called the Salton Sink. Instead he called the basin by the name we use today—Imperial Valley.

Settlers flocked into the desert basin with the beautiful name. The first of them found only a wasteland. Sand and salt flats burned under the sun. The tallest things between the men and the distant mountains were a few sickly mesquite trees and creosote bushes. But most of the land was owned by the Government and could be settled on without cost. The lure of free land and the promise of water "coming soon" drew people in by the thousands.

On May 14, 1901, the first red rush of water from the Colorado flowed through the feeder canals and within a few weeks the crops began to grow. The word spread and thousands more farmers flocked to the Imperial Valley. By 1904, 7,000 men and their families worked their own land happily. The Southern Pacific Railroad laid tracks into the Valley itself in order to carry new settlers in and farm produce out. Dozens of little towns sprung up, including one right on the Mexican border. The Mexican half of this town became known as Mexicali and the California side was called Calexico.

By this time everyone was making money. The farmers sold $700,000 worth of crops in 1904. The company owned by Rockwood and Chaffey charged the farmers $22 per acre to supply them with water, and had taken in more than $2 million. Even the Southern Pacific Railroad had bought land on the Mexican side of the border in the hope that it, too, could be irrigated and become valuable farm land.

Perhaps Chaffey knew that the Imperial Valley boom was headed for trouble. Or perhaps he was tired of running an irrigation business. Whatever his reasons were, he sold his interest in the water company to a group of men and left the Valley for good.

Almost as soon as he was gone, problems began to appear. The muddy water of the Colorado had dropped tons of sediment into the channel that Chaffey had built to water the dry riverbed. As the canal slowly choked with sediment, the flow of water into the Valley slowed and the crops began to die in the 100-degree heat.

Rockwood and his new partners looked for a way to open the channel. They decided that removing the plug of silt would take too long, so they dug a small ditch to connect the main irrigation canal with the river around the plug. They did not build a gate with which they could control the flow of water through the ditch because it was February. Everyone felt certain that they would be safe from high water until the snows melted in the spring. By then, surely the main channel would be cleared.

But the Colorado River did not cooperate with the people of Imperial Valley. High in the mountains, rain fell and snow melted. The Colorado ran bank-full toward the Gulf of California. With no flood gate to stop it, much of this water left the river and flowed through the temporary ditch, through the old riverbed, into Imperial Valley.

Rockwood was in Los Angeles when word reached him that water was rushing out of control through the irrigation canals. He hurried back to the Valley and found that the water had widened the new ditch to 60 feet. Twice he tried to close the break with dams of brush, logs, and sandbags. But both times the rushing, red flood tore the materials away. That was in March, 1905.

By June, the ditch had become 160 feet wide and 90,000 cubic feet of water was pouring into the basin each second. The water found its way through the irrigation ditches and across the new farmland to the deepest part of the Valley. There it began to collect and spread, forming a lake that later would be known as the Salton Sea. The helpless settlers watched the lake grow larger and larger, covering more and more farmland. If the flow of water into the Valley was not stopped, they realized, the entire basin might become one huge lake.

Rockwood's water company was rapidly going broke paying for the debris that was being thrown into the water only to be carried away by the current. In desperation, the owners of the company asked the Southern Pacific Railroad for help.

The managers of the railroad wanted to help stop the flood for several reasons. The success of the farmers in the Valley would provide the railroad with a lot of business, hauling produce to New Orleans and bringing people and supplies into the Valley. Also the railroad owned a huge tract of land in the desert just across the border in Mexico and this land could someday be turned into valuable farmland with water from the Imperial Valley irrigation system. And, of course, the railroad had laid a lot of tracks through the valley and, as the Salton Sea spread, these were being covered and had to be rebuilt elsewhere.

E. H. Harriman, President of the Southern Pacific Railroad, agreed to help. But he insisted on having control of the water in return for the money that it would take to control the flood. Rockwood and his friends agreed to this, and Harriman appointed a new man to head the water company. He was a civil engineer named Espes Randolph. Rockwood became the company's chief engineer. A former teacher of engineering, H. T. Cory, became Rockwood's assistant.

Together the three men tried to stop the flow of the river. They found that the Colorado no longer flowed across the delta to the Gulf of California. Instead, all of the water in the river now flowed into the Imperial Valley through the widened ditch and the old riverbed. By the fall of 1905, the Salton Sea covered 150 square miles of the basin's floor and was growing daily.

The men spent $60,000 of the railroad's money building another dam across the break in the river's bank. This dam had to be 600 feet long to reach across the ditch and it took almost all of the month of November to complete building it. Then, on the last day of November, a flash-flood smashed down the Gila River from somewhere in central Arizona. The Gila enters the Colorado River at Yuma, a short distance upstream from where the new dam had been built. The water in the larger river rose ten feet in ten hours and the new dam crumpled like paper under the pressure. More than 100,000 cubic feet of water poured through the gap each second for the next few hours, and when the water finally returned to its normal flow, no sign of the new dam could be found.

The three engineers—Rockwood, Randolph, and Cory—decided that a dam across the ditch was not possible and looked for other solutions. Rockwood showed them the original canal that had been choked with silt. He suggested that they design and build a huge, steam-driven dredge that could be used to remove the sediment from the canal. They could then build a new flood gate where the canal left the river. Once the flow of water from the river was turned into the original canal, the flow through the newer ditch would be smaller and could be dammed.

The other men agreed and the three went to San Francisco. There they found a company that could build a dredge that would do the job. Satisfied, they returned to the river to begin work on the new flood gate and wait for the delivery of the dredge, which had been promised by early summer.

It was early on the morning of April 18, 1906, in San Francisco. Many of the city's nearly 500,000 people were beginning to stir from their night's sleep. A few miles away, the rocks along the sides of a huge crack in the earth known as the San Andreas Fault shifted a few feet. Shock waves traveled out through the earth at two-miles-per-second and smashed through the city. For 75 seconds the earth shook and buildings collapsed on helpless people.

When the dust cleared, the survivors of the terrible earthquake found thousands of buildings lying in piles of rubble and hundreds of fires springing up all over San Francisco. Firemen trying to fight these fires discovered that the tremors in the earth had destroyed the water mains. The fires spread from block to block.

The waterfront was especially hard hit, both by the earthquake itself and by fires which burned unchecked there for 48 hours. The company that was building Rockwood's dredge was ruined beyond recovery and the dredge was completely destroyed. When this news reached Rockwood, he abandoned his dream of making the desert fertile and resigned from the company.

The Southern Pacific Railroad and Espes Randolph were now in complete control of the Imperial Valley water company. They were also completely responsible for the saving of the farms in the Valley. Randolph rushed to San Francisco to talk with President Harriman in the railroad's main office.

Harriman was faced with a tremendous job. His railroad had been badly damaged by the earthquake. Millions of dollars worth of trains, tracks, and buildings lay in total ruin, yet he knew that the victims of the catastrophe would rely upon the railroad for transportation out of the destroyed city and that those people who remained behind would need food and supplies that only the railroad could carry. In spite of this, he told Randolph to spend as much as another $250,000 on the flood in the Imperial Valley.

Cory, the former engineering teacher, was now in full charge of the work on the river. The late-spring floods, caused by the melting of the mountain snow, had started all along the Colorado and the Gila. Six billion cubic feet of water per day poured into the Valley through the break that was now half a mile wide. The Salton Sea in the northern end of the Valley covered an area of 400 square miles with water that was 60 feet deep in places, and it grew seven inches deeper each day. The twin towns of Calexico and Mexicali, sitting on the border at the southern end of the Valley, were three-fourths destroyed. Twelve thousand people were making preparations to abandon their farms forever.

Cory was determined to dam the flood once and for all this time. He and his friends had underestimated the strength of the flood before, so he laid his plans carefully. During the summer of 1906, the engineer gathered materials and men. As the spring floods slowed and the flow of water dropped, he built a trestle across the ditch. On this bridge he then laid railroad tracks. Tons and tons of rock were dug from every quarry within 400 miles of the Valley and loaded into huge side-dump railroad cars.

By August, everything was ready and Cory ordered the fourth attempt to dam the flood to begin. Three hundred of the dump cars, each carrying 60 tons of rock, rolled onto the trestle in train after train. The rocks were dumped over the side of the bridge and the dam grew quickly. The water flowing into the Imperial Valley slowed, became a trickle, and then stopped entirely.

Cory immediately went to work on the building of a huge flood gate, through which he could let a small amount of water flow into the valley. The farmers were happy that the flood had been stopped, but everyone knew that the farms could survive only if a steady flow of water for irrigation could be brought into the basin.

On October 11th, however, the Colorado River again reached flood stage. Cory stood on high ground above his dam and watched two-thirds of it and the new concrete flood gate lift upward on the current and wash away. For the next two weeks, more trains crossed the trestle that had somehow managed to withstand the first rush of water. Every engine in southern California and Arizona was sent to bring long trains of side-dump cars full of rock across the bridge. Most of the rock dumped into the swirling water washed away before it hit the bottom, but some remained and finally, on November 4, the dam was again solid.

This time, Cory did not stop pouring rocks into the ditch. By early December, the dam was high and strong, and ready for anything the Colorado could throw against it.

And the river tried. On December 7 a rush of water from the Gila River hit the dam furiously but could not move it. The water rushed southward across the delta, toward the Gulf.

But once on the soft silt of the delta, the tumbling water had something it could move. Steadily the current cut into the bank of the river south of the huge pile of rock. The course of the river slowly shifted to the west. A levee a half a mile south of Cory's dam was demolished and the water again broke from its banks. This time it cut a channel around the dam and found its way back into the ditch. Within a few hours, water was again flooding into the Valley through a break nearly 1,000 feet wide.

The Southern Pacific Railroad had spent nearly $2 million trying to stop the Colorado from flooding the Imperial Valley and the directors of the company decided that the Federal Government should help. Telegrams flashed back and forth between San Francisco and Washington. President Theodore Roosevelt was uncertain that the Federal Government had any business helping a railroad stop a flood without the permission of Congress. And Congress was about to take its Christmas vacation. President Roosevelt finally promised that when Congress returned to work he would ask for some money to reimburse the railroad for the expense of fighting this new flood. So, Cory was told to go back to work trying to dam the new break.

By now the engineer knew that it was possible to dam the flow from the river, if he could get enough rock into the channel. This time two trestles were built across the new break, and rails were laid on them. Rock was again hauled in, this time from as far away as 500 miles. When everything was ready, the dumping began. In the next 15 days, 3,000 of the huge side-dump cars rolled onto the bridges, dumped their 60-ton loads, and moved on.

This new pile of rock held and attention could turn again to the damage that the two years of floods had caused in the valley. The Salton Sea now

*Their dream of a farm in the Imperial Valley
lies drowned in water from
the rampaging Colorado River.*

covered 450 square miles of the basin floor. Deep gullies had been cut through many of the farms that had just begun to produce crops and the steady wind was again beginning to pile up the loose soil into huge dunes. Roads and railroad tracks lay under tons of loose rock and dirt. Loose boards on hundreds of deserted shacks rattled in the wind while buzzards wheeled overhead.

In Washington, President Roosevelt kept his promise and asked Congress to pay the Southern Pacific Railroad for the work they had done. At first Congress did not want to make what was called "a gift to a private company," but later $700,000 was paid to the railroad that had spent something over $3 million to fight the flood.

A few years later, the farmers of the Valley voted to form their own water company and bought the entire canal system. From this sale, the Southern Pacific Railroad received about $3 million and, therefore, recovered the money it had spent.

In 1936 work was finished on Hoover Dam, many miles upstream on the Colorado, not far from Grand Canyon. This dam, one of the highest in the world, finally had tamed the Colorado River. Now a steady flow of water is released daily from the dam. Downstream to the south, near the site of the old canal, stand the flood gates that protect the entrance to an irrigation canal built in 1940. Through the All-American Canal, as it is called, water flows to the irrigation feeder canals in the Imperial Valley. This newer irrigation system has finally turned the once-dry desert into a half a million acres of the most productive and beautiful farm land in America.

But to the north of these fertile acres lies a quiet reminder of those terrible two years of 1905 to 1907. Without an outlet to the ocean, the Salton Sea is still nearly 30 miles long and 10 miles wide and slowly evaporates in the hot desert sun.

CHAPTER NINE

BUFFALO HOLLOW 1972

AMON FINLEY HAD LIVED in the Appalachian Mountain valley known as Buffalo Hollow almost all of his life. An attack of polio at the age of three months had left him partly paralyzed. Because of this he did not work in the mines that dotted the sides of the hollow. With the help of a monthly check of $136 from his dead father's Social Security and through doing as much work as his crippled arm and leg would allow, he had managed to provide for his elderly mother and pay off most of the loans on two small houses.

The houses stood in the mining camp known as Lundale. The mountains crowded in close to the camp, forcing the houses into a single row between the road and the railroad tracks. Across the narrow blacktop road, perhaps 50 yards from Amon's front door, was the quiet little stream called Buffalo Creek.

Behind his houses were two of the many mines in the valley. These were both owned by the Amherst Coal Company. The entrances to the shafts were somewhere high up on the steep side of the mountain, lost in the thick trees. A long conveyor belt ran straight down the side of the mountain to the processing plant on the valley floor. These plants, called "tipples," formed a familiar jumble of corregated sheet iron, wires, ladders, and dirty grey smoke. Railroad cars almost always stood under the huge buildings, waiting to take on their loads of washed and sorted coal. Trains made up of 50 or more coal cars constantly traveled up and down the tracks behind Amon's houses, winding their way like huge black snakes through the nearly 20 miles of the hollow.

Even though Amon did not work for the coal company, he recognized the importance of the fossil fuel. West Virginia had for 40 years been the country's number one coal-producing state and only during the last year had it lost the championship to Kentucky. The coal deposits of Buffalo Hollow lay in the heart of Logan County, one of the main coal-producing areas in West Virginia.

Except for the little town of Man, standing at the mouth of the hollow where Buffalo Creek ran into the large Guyondot River, everything in the valley depended upon the coal mines. Not counting the 1,500 or so people who lived in Man, there were nearly 5,000 people living in 16 mining camps in Buffalo Hollow. This was more than the number of people who lived in the county seat of Logan, some 15 miles downstream on the Guyondot River.

Five hundred people were crowded into the camp of Lundale, and these were the people that Amon Finley called his neighbors. The Amherst Coal Company owned the only large buildings in the camp—two office buildings and a company store. The coal company even ran the only gasoline station in the camp.

In the 12 miles between Lundale and Man, were 11 separate mining camps. In these 11 communities lived 3,850 people. In the six miles of the valley that lay above Amon's houses there were only three camps—Lorado, Pardee, and Saunders. Lorado was the largest of the three, with a population of about 500. Pardee and Saunders were small camps of only about 100 people each. At the head of the valley, some seven miles above Lundale, stood the tipple of the Buffalo Mining Company.

Two generations of men had taken coal from the mines at the end of Buffalo Hollow. During the years of World War II, when coal had been needed more than it is today, the mines had been owned by the Lorado Coal Mining Company. The old shaft mines could not produce coal quickly enough for the steel furnaces that were busily making tanks and ships for use in the war, so the company began to strip mine the hills at the very top of the valley.

To do this, it was necessary to remove tons of slate and other useless rock in order to uncover the beds of valuable coal. The miners call this useless rock *slag*. To get the slag out of the way it was dumped into a small valley that runs into Buffalo Hollow near its head. Huge piles of the loose rock soon filled one part of the smaller valley and the tributary stream began to back up, forming a long lake. Unlike a cement dam, this slag heap had no valves that could be used to gradually release water into the stream below.

After the war, the mines were bought by the Buffalo Mining Company. By this time, the lake behind the slag dam had grown very large. In addition to water from streams, it was also made up of water that had seeped into mine shafts and had to be pumped out. By 1972, an estimated 360,000 gallons of water were being pumped into the lake from the mines. And, because the strip mining had taken so many trees from the steep hillsides, more and more water flowed into the lake along the surface of the ground.

Amon Finley had never visited the lake, but some of his neighbors had. There were actually three lakes at the head of the valley, they told him. There were two small lakes near the road and a large one farther back up the valley. The large lake stood quite a distance from the Buffalo Mine tipple, and no one really knew exactly how big it was. The slag

dam that held back the large lake had grown steadily through the years until it now stood well over
100 feet high in the middle. A few people in the
valley had managed to get boats into the lake and
had reported that in some places the winding arms
of water ran for several miles back into the mountains.

Some of the teenagers of Buffalo Hollow tried to
swim in the lake but soon gave it up. The water was
sour with the sulfuric acid that formed when the
coal was washed, and only a few feet below the
surface the water was black and thick with coal
dust. Besides, they said, the lake was terribly deep.
No one was able to hold his breath long enough to
find the bottom.

Many people who lived in the narrow hollow
below the lake were afraid that the dam might
break some day. Warnings that this was going to
happen were common, but in more than 30 years
the dam had not broken, and so very few people
were really concerned. Amon Finley hardly ever
thought about the lake. His mother had died
around the middle of January and the crippled
man was trying now to rebuild his life. After so
many years of taking care of his mother, he found
that he suddenly had little to do. Much of his time
was spent repairing the house she had lived in, in
the hopes that he could rent it to someone.

He woke up early on the morning of Saturday,
February 26, 1972. At about seven o'clock he went
out to inspect the new porch he had just built. It
was the biggest porch in all of Lundale—18 feet

long and 12 feet wide. It was made of four-inch-thick concrete, reinforced with steel rods. He was proud of his work and was glad that the winter weather had warmed up enough to let him finish the job.

The mountains in the southern part of West Virginia had been covered by snow for much of the winter, but now all of that was suddenly gone. A few days before, the temperature had climbed up and up until it almost felt like spring. A lot of warm rain had fallen, but not enough to concern the people of Buffalo Hollow.

People living farther downstream were more concerned about the rain. The Guyondot River was running bank-full at Man and had topped the 26-foot-deep mark on the bridges at Logan the day before. This was more than five feet below the record set in 1963, but it was bad enough. The lower two streets of Logan's business section were badly flooded, roads and bridges were awash, and the schools had been dismissed early for the weekend.

One man knew how big the lake above the hollow was and that the warm rain had washed the melting snow from the mountainsides into the lake. He was Deputy Sheriff Otto Mutters. A phone call at 5:30 on Saturday morning started him on his way up the hollow. The report was that the water behind the big dam was within a foot of the top of the slag pile. Mutters knew that the loose rock could not stand for long if the water started running over the top. He drove to the mine tipple at the head of the hollow. An official of the mine there told him that the dam was in good shape, but Mutters was not convinced. For the next two hours the deputy drove up and down the hollow, warning the people there that the dam might break. But few of them listened to him.

"I didn't know how much water was up there," Amon Finley explained later. "If I had known, I'd have got out right then."

Other people tried to warn Amon and his neighbors. At 7:10 a.m., an employee of the mining company took a look at the dam and called his mother on the two-way radio in his truck.

"The dam is going to go," he warned her. "Get out of there now and warn as many people as you can."

The woman quickly gathered up what she could and left for the safety of the hillside. She passed the warning on to her next door neighbor, who in turn passed it on to Amon as he stood admiring his new front porch. But the man still did not believe that he was in any danger and went back into his house.

Other employees of the mining company had realized that the dam was in dangerous condition. A group of them decided at about 7:00 a.m. that the valley should be evacuated. They formed a long parade of cars and began making their way down from the mine, blowing their horns and flashing their lights.

Just below the dam stood the cluster of houses called Saunders. At a couple of minutes after 8:00 a.m., the electricity went off and someone shouted a warning.

"Run for your lives!"

But there wasn't time for most of the people of Saunders. From their houses they watched helplessly as the small dam that held back the lake nearest them gave way. They heard a terrible roar as 20 million cubic feet of water pushed through the narrow opening. A church was wrenched from its foundations and floated toward them. A wall of water from the large dam farther up the valley topped the smaller dams and crushed the houses like toys.

Cars streamed in all directions as the desperate people tried to get to higher ground. One family spent precious minutes trying to catch their dog and the water was waist deep before they finally got to their car. A man with only one leg lost first one crutch and then the other in the swirling water and finally had to crawl up the steep hillside. A car bounced down the railroad tracks in an effort to get closer to the side of the mountain. The water stripped the bedrock bare of soil as it roared through the mining camp.

The water wiped out the few houses of Saunders and smashed through Pardee without warning. This camp was wiped clean of everything but the biggest cottonwood trees. By this time the flood was a wall of tumbling, black water nearly 40 feet high,

The houses that once were a part of a mining camp in West Virginia's Buffalo Hollow lie jumbled together in scattered piles. ▶

bouncing from wall to wall of the valley. Fortunately for the people farther down the hollow, the valley floor is not steep and the thick water moved down it at what must have been only about 20 miles an hour.

The homes of the 500 people living at Lorado were demolished next. Railroad tracks were torn from their ties and bent double. Railroad cars of coal, weighing more than 50 tons, were rolled like toys in a bathtub.

The torrent rushed down on Lundale. In spite of the warnings that he had gotten, Amon Finley was back in his house, standing near a second story window. He heard a roaring sound, and looked up the valley.

"It looked like a big, old, black wall coming," he said later. "I could see that it was carrying houses along with it."

As fast as his crippled leg would carry him, he rushed down the stairs and out of the house. Without thinking, he gathered up the jacket he had thrown on a chair near the front door. He ran down the valley, away from the tumbling water, around the side of a neighbor's house, across the railroad tracks, and scrambled up the steep slope to safety.

"The water was right behind me all the way. I usually can't run very fast, but I'll tell you that I was really moving that day!"

From the side of the mountain, Amon looked back into his valley. The black water seemed to pick up his houses and toss them into the air. Then the wall of water poured over them and smashed them to bits. The heavy cement porch that he had worked on for so long lifted in the current like a raft and floated downstream. His prize apple trees bent with the force of the water and then were ripped out by the roots. A telephone pole snapped like a twig.

The 12-year-old son of a family that lived a few houses down from Amon had been playing in the back of an old pickup truck. The truck was parked in the lot near the company store in Lundale. The boy looked up and saw the water coming. Realizing what had happened, he started to run for the mountainside. But then he remembered his mother and father at home, and knew that they did not know that they were in danger. Quickly he ran back up the valley, directly toward the black wall of water. Wading through water up to his knees, he managed to warn his parents in time for them all to escape. But their home and everything in it was washed away.

At the camp called Stowe, a family heard the noise and saw what looked to them to be a huge cloud rolling down the valley. Without taking time to put on shoes, they left the house and plunged into water that was up to their knees. While they struggled through the water, their house was torn apart and from the safety of a hill side they watched their car being lifted up and thrown onto the pile of rubble that had been their home.

Here, at the place where Stowe stood, the valley begins to widen out. You might expect that the water would have spread out here and lost much of its force. But a metal bridge, its sign announcing that it could hold a weight of 12,000 pounds, was torn from its foundations and carried downstream for several yards. There it stuck, and tons of broken houses, cars, and bodies piled up behind it.

At Crites, the valley narrows again, and here the water swept all signs of life away. Then it spilled out into another broad place in the valley. By the time it reached Amhersdale, the mid-point in the valley, the flood was nearly 500 yards across and still 20 feet deep. The main current of the river was strong enough to carry away or damage 32 of 37 houses standing alongside the creek bed, but the water killed very few people below this point. And, by the time it reached Man, the flood did not damage strong buildings at all. But it carried tons of black mud into almost every home and building. Many of these had to be abandoned later because the walls were full of the slimy silt.

Back in the hollow, the people began coming down out of the mountains. Amon Finley returned to Lundale to find that nothing remained of his two houses, not even the foundations. Uninsured against flood, his life savings of $18,000 were gone. Worse than this, the bodies of his neighbors lay sprawled in the mud and hung from the trees in all directions. Those who had survived felt thankful to be alive, even though they owned nothing but the clothing they wore. The rain suddenly began to feel quite cold. Except for the company store and one other building, Lundale was gone.

Help began to arrive quickly. Rescue teams from Man began walking up the hollow almost as soon as the splintered wreckage reached the town. Helicopters fluttered over the ruined hollow, and police cars sat sideways across the road, their red lights reflecting on the piles of debris.

It was Sunday before Amon Finley was taken aboard a helicopter. The clattering machine flew first to the head of the valley to pick up two more survivors from the wreckage of Saunders. From the air, Amon looked down on the smashed valley.

For the only time in his life he saw the dams—three piles of black gravel, each with a huge hole torn from its center. He saw the valley floor littered with the wreckage of hundreds of homes, smashed cars, overturned railroad cars, and twisted railroad tracks. He watched men scramble up the sides of the mountains, trying to reach the bodies that sometimes hung 30 feet above the now-quiet stream. And everywhere he saw that everything was covered with a black slime that would later dry into a thick layer of coal dust.

The helicopter took its passengers down the valley and landed on the football field of Man High School. The pilot told the three to report to the Red Cross center in the field house. There they found many people ready to help them find temporary shelter, warm clothing, and something to eat.

The town was already full of soldiers. Troop I of the West Virginia National Guard had been called into action and had taken over the problem of searching the valley for survivors. Nearly 1,500.

people were reported as missing, and a steady stream of trucks and helicopters brought bodies to the temporary morgue set up in the Plainview Grade School.

The need for food and drinkable water farther up the hollow was becoming a serious problem. In the ruins of Lorado, more than 500 people had gathered and needed help. Another 500 workers had come into the valley, and these people also needed food and water. Huge, double-rotared helicopters of the U. S. Army soon began to carry heavy freight into the hollow. Water purification units were flown in from the U. S. Army post at Ft. Bragg, North Carolina. Salvation Army mobile kitchens from as far away as Washington, D. C., were seen handing out free food in the ruins of three camps.

Groups of Mennonites from Virginia and Pennsylvania began to arrive by the carload. Trained by the Virginia flood of 1969, these volunteers quickly organized themselves into search-and-rescue teams.

On Monday, seven more bodies were dug from the debris and added to the 60 people who already lay in the morgue. The names of 250 missing people were posted throughout the valley and appeared in every newspaper in the state. Relatives of the missing fearfully inspected each body as it was brought into the morgue.

On Wednesday the body of a woman was found in the Guyondot River nearly 100 miles downstream from the broken dams. She was covered

with the slimy, black mud that stained everything
in Buffalo Hollow. This discovery brought the
total of known dead to 72.

Heavy earthmoving equipment was now being
brought into the hollow. Bulldozers, front-end
loaders, trucks, and tractors probed the debris and
moved tons of dirt and rocks. A steady rain poured
down on the rescue teams, but the temperature was
warm during the daylight hours. From the
smashed houses piled against the bridge at Stowe,
the Mennonites pulled the bodies of two small children. By Saturday morning, a full week after the
dam burst, 85 bodies had been found and 120 people were still missing. No one dared guess what the
final death toll would be.

It seemed that the hollow was beginning to recover somewhat. A path had been pushed through
the debris to the very end of the valley, roughly
following the course of the old road. None of the
bridges were still standing, of course, but the bed of
Buffalo Creek had been cleared and trucks could
easily ford it when it was necessary. Piles of debris
had been carefully searched and were burning in a
chilly March wind. Seven Salvation Army canteens
served food and drinks to the hundreds of people
who worked in spite of the cold rain. Mobile homes
owned by the U. S. Government had begun to arrive and electric power was again available to the
lower parts of the valley.

By the end of another week it looked as if Buffalo Hollow would quickly return to normal. The
National Guard troops had left. The mines as far

up the valley as Lorado had started operations again and many of the men were able to bring home regular paychecks. Three hundred people were still without homes, but the Government officials promised that mobile homes would arrive before the end of the month. No more bodies were being found, in spite of the fact that 51 people were still reported missing. The Mennonites were again busy carrying mud from the houses that still stood, and the sounds of their hammers and saws filled the cold air.

But something went wrong. Buffalo Hollow did not return to normal. A year and a half later the scars of the flood were still to be seen everywhere. The road above Lorado was still not repaired. People still lived in Government-owned mobile homes and only a few houses were being built to replace those destroyed by the water.

Arguments as to who was responsible for the disaster went on and on. At least one national magazine called it "murder." The mining company that owned the dam claimed that the state government refused to allow them to release water from the lake. The company also claimed the flood was "an act of God."

"The State was more concerned over the welfare of the fish in the river than they were in the welfare of the people," an official of the mining company said. "Now both the fish and the people are gone. The dam simply wasn't able to hold all of the water that God put into the lake."

State officials, on the other hand, claimed that they could find no request from the mining company to release water from the lake. But apparently the State Inspectors had not looked at the dam for more than 14 months before the disaster occurred.

As the arguments went on, the people who still lived in Buffalo Hollow tried to rebuild their lives. Some left the hollow forever, of course. Others remained, but lived in constant fear. In the spring, when the heavy rains came, some mothers refused to send their children to school and fathers refused to leave their families, even to go to work. Some of the people slept in their clothes, while others sat on their porches throughout the night, watching the river.

On February 25, 1973, one year after the disaster, a memorial service was held in the Man High School Field House. Listed on the back page of the Order of Service were the names of 114 known dead. In the cemetery are four headstones marked "unknown." About 20 people were still unaccounted for.

During this memorial service, the survivors of the flood remembered the tragedy. They also tried to find something to be thankful for.

"We are not the same as we were a year ago," the Reverend Ralph Thompson said, "because we have experienced suffering, loss, sorrow, frustration, and anger which have left their marks upon us. In some ways we are stronger; in some ways we are weaker.

"We are grateful for neighbors and friends," he continued, "who have shared with us during these difficult days and who remain by our side this day."

Among the people who stayed "by the side" of the people of Buffalo Hollow were teams of workers from the Mennonite Disaster Service (MDS). Among the first of the rescuers were the black-bearded Mennonites from Virginia and Pennsylvania. Among them was Jonas Kanagy, about whom you read earlier in this book.

After the bodies were recovered and the houses cleared, another type of Mennonite began to arrive. These men and women were from Ohio, Illinois, and Indiana. Few wore the traditional dark clothing and none of the men had spade-shaped beards. These were skilled craftsmen and trained social workers, and they had come to stay until the people of Buffalo Hollow were back on their feet.

An example of this "new" type of Mennonite is Ralph Sommer, whom we met in the summer of 1973, a year and a half after the flood. He wears his graying hair long and has heavy sideburns. Instead of the beard I had come to expect, he wears a bushy mustache. Trained in social work, he works with his wife who is an experienced teacher. Also on the MDS team is a retired building contractor and 12 volunteers of high school and college age.

The eight boys and four girls who made up the summer work team came from as far away as Canada. They paid their own transportation into Logan County and received $15 per month spending money, food, and room. Most of them were Mennonites, but Sommer said that he would be happy to have any volunteer who wanted to work.

The main job of the group after the flood was the repair and rebuilding of houses. At first this was a disappointment to Sommer.

"I thought that we were going to be able to build quite a few new homes," he said. "But the state is trying to build a bigger highway through the hollow and no one wants to build a home on land that might be taken for a right-of-way.

"However, I think now that it has been good for our young people to work primarily on rebuilding. Instead of getting into only four or five homes this summer, they have been able to get into 20 or 30. This has given them a chance to learn a lot about people whose life style is very much different from their own.

"I have encouraged our young people to take the time to sit and talk with the people of the hollow. This is good for the local people. It gives them a chance to talk out their problems. And it helps our kids to understand the feelings and frustrations of others. They have come to understand themselves a little better, I think. They get to compare their own values and ideas with very much different kinds of values and ideas."

The Mennonite team lived and worked out of five mobile homes supplied free by the U. S. Government. On the other side of the trailer park was another group of young volunteers, this one sponsored by the Quakers. Working closely together, the two groups learned how to share their abilities and time with people who are in need.

"Right after the flood, it was easy to see the desperate needs of the people here," Sommer said. "It is easy to throw yourself into the job of cleaning mud out of someone's house. It is a little more difficult to understand the need that a family might have for an extra bedroom, even when there are 14 people in a house with only four rooms. Our young people have come to see that eight people sleeping in the same bedroom is a crisis, just as much as having mud in the house."

The Mennonites planned to stay in Buffalo Hollow at least through the summer of 1974, and Sommer felt that they might have to stay even longer. He saw a great need for legal aid, family guidance, and child-care centers.

"We hope to be able to work through the local churches, rather than as Mennonites. The needs of the people here are going to continue for a long, long time. We hope that we can help set up a local organization that can do the job."

CHAPTER TEN

FLOODS: THEIR CAUSES AND CONTROL

THROUGHOUT THE HISTORY of the earth, floods have plagued mankind. No part of the earth, except the highest land, seems to be entirely safe from floods. Even in the dryest deserts water rushes down normally dry gulleys once in a while, washing away anything that man has been foolish enough to put in its path.

In the United States alone, during an average year, 80 people are drowned in flood waters. An average of 75,000 Americans must leave their homes each year to escape floods.

As you have seen from what you have read in this book, floods may be caused by many different things. Perhaps the most common causes of floods are heavy rainfalls or deep snows that melt more quickly than normal. Dams may break and cause the valleys below them to be suddenly under water. Or a hurricane may push high storm waves across a beach and cause a flood on the land beyond. Other severe floods along the ocean shoreline may be caused by the dreaded *tsunami* waves, which in turn are caused by underwater earthquakes or volcanoes.

But often the real cause of a flood is man. Because of his desire to make money quickly or through his lack of understanding of the way nature works, man tries to change the normal course that water follows across the land. He builds dams. He changes the course of the rivers. And he builds his homes, cities, and factories in areas that are known to be in danger of flooding.

At first, it seems logical that man should settle along the flood plains of rivers, where the danger of flooding is the worse. The floods of the past have enriched the soil of the valleys by dropping tons of rich soil along either side of the river's channel. And the river itself provides water for man's use in dozens of ways—from drinking water to a free method of transportation. But the floods that have washed over the land of the river's valley will come again and again, and the cost can be tremendous.

Floods may vary greatly in size, sometimes covering only a few acres and at other times inundating

millions of acres of farm land and towns. The size
of the flood makes little difference to the people
caught in it. To the family who has just seen everything they owned washed away, it is of little conso-
lation to know that thousands of other people have
suffered in the same way.

The most damaging floods in the United States
are caused by too much rainfall. A typical flood of
this type usually starts with a long period of fairly
steady rain. When the rain first begins, very little of
it finds its way into the streams. Instead, most of the
rainfall is at first caught by the vegetation on the
land and absorbed by the soil.

As the rain continues to fall, some of the water
that has soaked into the soil reaches the streams
through seepage. Eventually the soil becomes saturated with water and can hold no more. At this
point, any rain that falls will run across the surface
of the ground, downhill, and into the streams.

High in the mountains, the small streams move
swiftly and cut deep-sided, V-shaped valleys. Their
channels are more or less straight, turning only
when they run against a large mass of rock that
cannot be cut through. Flash floods along the banks
of these types of streams are common, but usually
do little damage, since the water is usually not deep
enough to get out of the deep-sided valley.

As the water in these small streams moves down
the side of the mountains it is joined by water from
other streams. Eventually a river is formed. The
river, running over more flat land than do the
mountain streams, does not move very fast and

may carve a winding path across a broad flood plain. From all over the river's watershed, a number of tributary streams may add more water into the main channel.The water in the big river grows deeper and spills over its natural banks, quickly spreading out over the flat flood plain on either side of the channel.

This fast-moving water carries with it particles of soil washed from the hillsides. When it begins to move more slowly, the soil is deposited on the flood plains. Much of the best farmland in the United States lies there in the natural flat land beside the rivers. Perhaps as much as 50 million acres of our country are flat lowlands, bordering rivers. It has been estimated that more than ten million Americans live on these plains and are therefore exposed to the dangers of floods almost anytime it rains upriver from where they live. Damage to property standing in these areas now runs into the billions of dollars each year.

Scientists, engineers, government officials, and many other people spend their lives trying to protect these people from the dangers of floods. The problem is being attacked from many different directions: control, prediction and warning, and relief and rehabilitation for the victims.

The great hope of everyone who lives in an area threatened by floods is that someday we will learn how to prevent the rivers from damaging property and people. There are many state and federal programs aimed at doing just this. There are also attempts to prevent people from building homes and living in dangerous areas. The trouble with these attempts is that the flood plains of our major rivers contain rich soil the farmer wants to own. The land along the rivers is flat and builders find it cheaper to construct buildings there than in the mountains. With water nearby, the manufacturer finds it profitable to put factories on the flood plain. Thus, it is difficult to keep people out of these potentially dangerous areas.

Other programs set up standards for construction of buildings in areas that might flood. Ways are being found to build houses and larger buildings so that they will not easily float off their foundations during a flood. Electric wires and appliances can be made in such ways that they will not be damaged by being submerged. Waterproof coverings for windows and doors are being made, and these can be installed to protect a building during flood times. Buildings on huge cement pillars are now seen in some flood plains, with their offices—and thus their valuable papers—high above possible flood depths.

Throughout the history of civilized man, attempts have been made to prevent the rivers from leaving their channels. The construction of levees, dikes, flood walls, and the like is the most common way this has been done. In all parts of the world, large rivers are lined with high, man-made walls of dirt, sandbags, and cement. Levees help solve the problem somewhat, but they create other problems. Holding a flooding river inside high levees increases the speed of the water and this, in turn, causes the water to erode away the banks of the river at a faster rate. And, when a levee is overtopped, the result is a sudden flooding of the low land behind the wall, sometimes without warning to the people living there.

Another method of preventing the river from leaving its channel is to make the natural riverbed wider, deeper, and straighter. At first, this seems to work fairly well, especially when combined with a system of levees. However, once a riverbed has been made bigger and straighter, it is usually necessary to continue to dredge sediment from it. This can be a very costly method of flood control and one that must be continued forever.

Have you ever gone camping and dug a ditch around your tent? This is an example of a third way of preventing rivers from flooding. The idea here is to give the flood waters another channel to run into before it can flood into an area inhabited by people. There are several such alternate channels along the Mississippi River. When the river becomes dangerously full of water, the extra water can be channeled through other stream beds which relieves the threat of flood farther downstream.

Huge dams have been built all over the world in attempts to prevent floods. The dams block the natural flow of the rivers and hold their water in huge lakes. Thus, when a heavy flow of water comes down the river, it can be held and released at a later time. The lakes behind such dams have other values beyond their use in flood control. We use many of these lakes for recreational areas, water supplies for towns and industries, and for irrigation of farm lands below the dams. The water rushing through openings at the base of the dam can also be used to generate electricity. There are problems, of course. Sediment that normally would have flowed on down the river collects behind these dams and eventually fills up the lake. And, the building of such dams must result in the permanent drowning of many acres of farm and woodlands. Too, there is always the possibility that the dam will break and cause tremendous flooding downstream.

The last method of trying to prevent flood water from leaving the river channel is careful management of the land in the river's watershed. Since much of the water that enters the river came to it over the surface of the land, scientists have tried to find ways to lower the amount of runoff. One way to do this is to keep the soil carefully planted with a heavy cover of vegetation. Another way is to build small ponds to catch and hold the heavy runoff of water. In these ways, the water is held until it can soak into the soil, rather than run off into the streams.

But in spite of all of these programs, rivers continue to flood and people continue to suffer. In order to protect us from damaging floods it is necessary that floods be predicted and that warnings be sent out to people who may be in their paths.

The prediction of floods is a highly scientific business. It begins with the National Weather Service

and the scientists who study the weather. Using
highly complicated equipment, such as airplanes,
radar, and satellites, these scientists watch the
weather all over the world. Using the data they
gather, the weather men try to predict when and
where it will rain and how much water will fall.

Engineers who have studied the flood patterns of
a particular river basin watch the river carefully.
Measurements are made of the water level all along
the length of the river, from the mountain streams
to the ocean.

Forecasts of what the river might do are carefully
prepared. If it appears that the river might reach
its flood stage, warnings are sent out. Such warnings, if accurate, can save many lives and allow
people time to move valuable property to safer
ground.

But the science of weather and flood forecasting
is not 100 percent accurate, and some floods do
catch people unaware. Even when there is enough
warning, many people do not leave the threatened
area. Or, if they do leave, they often must leave
their property behind.

In every flood there are victims who are in need
of relief and rehabilitation. After a flood strikes,
the first need of the people in the damaged area is
to be rescued from the flood water. People are
often stranded in the upper floors of their homes,
on the roofs of buildings, on hills that have become
islands, or even in the branches of trees or the cross-
arms of telephone poles. While the flood is still
raging it is necessary for other people to come to

the rescue of these stranded victims. Since this need comes early in the flood, it is usually up to local people to do this rescue work. Fire and police departments, civil defense units, military units, and individuals go out in boats and helicopters to save these lives.

Even before the water reaches a community many people will have heard the warnings and moved from their homes. As the water rises, more and more displaced people will join the first refugees. These people must find shelter, food, water, and sometimes clothing. If the weather is bad, these necessities must be supplied quickly. Children and old people have special needs that must be met. Early in the disaster the problems must be handled by local organizations, such as civil defense or local church groups. Later such organizations as the Red Cross and Salvation Army may help.

After the water level drops, someone must wade through the mud and debris in order to search for the dead and injured. Bodies must be taken to a morgue, identified, and buried. The injured must be gotten to hospitals quickly and safely. It is up to local people—people who know the damaged area well—to coordinate these search-and-rescue operations. But much of the actual work may be taken over by people from the outside. Teams of Mennonites may arrive. Rescue squads, firemen, and policemen from nearby communities often come to help. National Guardsmen and military personnel are usually on their way as soon as word of the disaster is received. But someone from civil defense or the local police must be able to direct the work of these volunteers. And some groups, such as the Red Cross, the Salvation Army, or local organizations must provide food and shelter for these workers.

Throughout the flood, the workmen of the local utility companies and the local government are busy trying to restore electric power, telephone service, and fuel supplies. Within a few days after flood waters subside, the bodies of the dead and the injured have to be removed from the debris and attention given to damaged property. Work then must begin on cleaning and rebuilding the homes and businesses caught by the water. The owners of the property may be able to do this for themselves, but often they are too shocked by the experience they have been through to be able to help themselves. Usually it is necessary for someone from the outside to come in and help them get started. They not only need help in carrying out the mud and rebuilding their buildings, they also need money. If their homes are too badly damaged, it is sometimes necessary to buy materials for new ones.

If a disaster has been a large one, a great number of state and federal agencies, local organizations, and national relief groups will be available to help. Low-interest loans and rent-free mobile homes may be supplied by the federal government. Mudding-out and rebuilding is usually done by such groups as the Mennonite Disaster Service, working under the direction of the Red Cross. Local and state governments can supply help in various forms.

Sooner or later the Red Cross and the Salvation Army move on to new disaster sites, and the officers of the U.S. government agencies leave. But the people of the destroyed area will still need help. Perhaps their local industries have been badly damaged and many people are out of work. Sometimes people develop mental illnesses because of the experiences they have had and are in need of professional help. Often children are orphaned and need to be cared for. And many times, so much valuable property has been destroyed that the area cannot afford to pay the taxes necessary to rebuild its schools, roads, and water and sewer systems.

You may never be caught in a flood, but over the next 50 years some four million Americans will be. An understanding of floods, their causes and prevention, may help you to save the life of one of these people.

ACKNOWLEDGEMENTS

Photographs in this book are reproduced courtesy of the following:

pages 2–3, 9, 23, 107: New York Public Library
pages 48, 49: Italian Cultural Institute, New York
pages 55, 148–149: Wide World Photos
pages 65, 72 (bottom): U.S. Geological Survey, Water Resources Division
pages 71, 72 (top), 73: The Kansas State Historical Society, Topeka
page 113: Walter R. Brown
pages 136–137: The Bancroft Library

INDEX

About the Authors

Walter R. Brown has his Ph.D. in science education from The Ohio State University and enjoys teaching junior high school students. He has co-authored a science textbook series that is used in many junior high school science courses throughout the country.

Billye Walker Cutchen maintains a furious schedule of activity to keep up with all her interests. When she's not researching and writing about historical catastrophes, she edits other peoples' book manuscripts. Mrs. Cutchen keeps in touch with young people through her three teenage daughters and their friends.